THE HUMMINGBIRD
From
RESOLUTE

Memoirs of a Journey to the Polar Sea

David C. Whyte

First published, 1997
Revised and expanded, 2014
Additional edits, 2025

Comments or inquiries about this book may be directed to:
hbirdfromrez@gmail.com

Also in print by the author: *An Introduction to Michipicoten Island: Lake Superior's Wild Heart*

Maps: David C. Whyte
Photographs: David C. Whyte, Chris Morris, Christy Simpson

Cataloguing in Publication Data

Whyte, David C.
The hummingbird from Resolute: memoirs of a journey to the polar sea

ISBN 978-0-9689099-2-8

1. Whyte, David (David C.) -- Journeys --- Canada
2. Northwest Territories, Nunavut - Description and Travel
3. Recreational Canoeing - Subarctic Canada
Includes bibliographical references

To Jill and Christy, whose good humour and hard work did much to ensure that we reached our destination and to Chris, our leader and provider, whose boundless ego was matched only by his enthusiasm and ability. This journal is also dedicated to my family, friends and co-workers, whose moral support and encouragement enabled me to cast aside my doubts and boldly go.

There are few experiences more interesting to a traveller than to set out from a known point to trace what lies beyond. When the distant headland or far range is reached, there is a keenness to see what the new view will disclose. There may be disappointments, success or failure may follow, but always the new course is entered upon with eagerness.

Guy H. Blanchet, Canadian Explorer and Mapmaker (1884-1966).

Contents

List of Illustrations

Preface and Disclaimer

Before jumping into a strange canoe, it's a good idea to know where it's going and who's sitting at the other end. If you read this book, we'll be paddling companions for over 1,400 kilometres. I offer these words of preparation while there's still time to reconsider.

First, this journal isn't a seminar on wilderness paddling. There are no long-winded, technical expositions on draws, braces, riffles or eddies; no breathless testaments to the Zen of paddling, or becoming "one with the canoe." I said rude things to my boat during the many gruelling portages, and probably subjected it to unnecessary abuse. My observations on the art of the paddle, the simple musings of a newly minted voyageur, won't impress the grizzled veteran.

Those expecting weighty discourse on the fragile biology of the north will also be disappointed. I'll certainly tell you what we saw: wolves, muskoxen, mosquitoes and all, but without pithy pontificating on ecosystems or wildlife. We didn't keep a bird list. To the best of my knowledge, there was no running with the caribou or dozing naked on the tundra. We were too tired for the former, and the latter would have tempted too many black flies.

Although canoes and the environment are prominently featured because they dominated our summer so completely, this journal is primarily a daily record of events and introspections from a memorable journey with three friends: 55 days by paddle and portage from Yellowknife to the Arctic Ocean. If you want to know what the trip was really like, how it was accomplished, what worked and what didn't, read further. Equipment, food, logistics, biting insects, human drama, and what happened when the toilet paper got wet, you'll know it all. I've also included maps, photos and historical context for those who, like me, are lost without a frame of reference.

Get ready to work. We didn't drift down the long, wide Mackenzie River. We took an inside passage, paddling, dragging and slogging along and between rocky, disjointed lakes and streams, as we traversed the wind-blown tundra of the subarctic plateau. After paddling the length of Great Slave Lake, our course took us first northeast, then northwest, then northeast again, tracing an ill-formed, backwards "Z" on a map of Canada north of 60 degrees, like the mark of Zorro etched by a child. It wasn't all sunshine and rainbows, and I haven't tried to disguise any of the missteps, pain or drudgery. Neither have I tried to exaggerate the highlights that made the trip so memorable. The lows and highs are presented as they occurred, neither diminished nor embellished. I think the story is one worth sharing, and I took considerable pains to write it down. It would have been much easier just to close my eyes and sleep after crawling into the tent each night. I hope you'll find it was worth the effort, but that's for you to decide. As you read, consider this: others have gone farther and accomplished more, but this is a trip that you could do, with the right amount of forethought and preparation. Maybe you'll find inspiration in these pages.

Those who notice such things may worry that the units of measurement are a heady mixture of metric, for distances and speed, and imperial, for heights, weights and temperatures. Don't fret; it's just a reflection of the various maps and instruments consulted. The reader is free to convert the units as desired.

Finally, it's worth noting that my fellow travellers reviewed this journal to make sure I made no blatant errors of fact. Any errors of opinion or attitude must remain my own.

Chapter 1: ARCTIC HO!

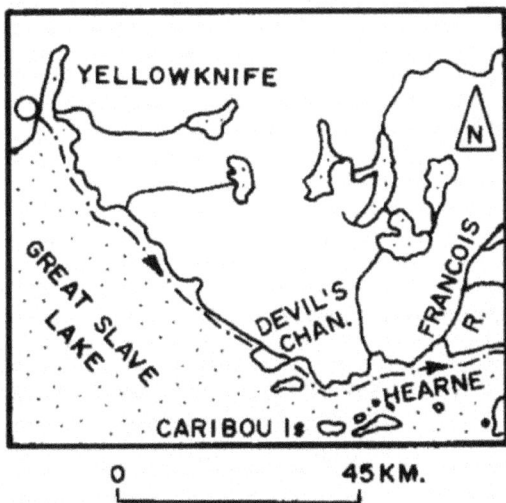

July 2

There are many places I might have chosen to begin this account: the preparations in Toronto last fall or the warm-up canoe trips this spring, for example. Instead, I choose to start in the women's clothing department of the Wal-Mart in Yellowknife, for it's here that I first begin to realize the personal significance of what I'm about to undertake along with my three companions, Jill, Christy and Chris. As I look around at the varied trappings of madcap consumerism, I feel a fierce surge of joy that I am soon to become, at least for a short while, free of it all. A superior man in an inferior setting, I cast my eyes about with the snooty, idealistic disdain only those temporarily exempted from society's daily obligations and routines can generate.

I do buy one thing: a floppy, wide-brimmed women's golf hat of white cotton, tastefully trimmed in green. I'm not usually a cross-dresser or a slave to female fashion; it's just that I can't find any suitable men's hats. The typical baseball style on offer would shade my eyes, but leave my ear tips out to fry in the glint and glare of Great Slave Lake. With the golf hat in place, my ears are nowhere to be seen. Even allowing for future shrinkage, it should do the trick. A Tilley-style hat would also work, but they are expensive, and our leader, Chris, for reasons he doesn't share, has banned them from the expedition. So, I make my hurried purchase while Jill and Christy buy some last-minute goodies for our food supply, and Chris makes a few calls from the pay phone at the front of the store.

Next stop is the McDonald's restaurant across the street, a secular shrine instinctively visited by many about to forsake civilized convenience in favour of some greater, wilder calling. Maybe it's the modern-day equivalent of outbound Northwest Company voyageurs pausing at the chapel of Notre Dame de Bon Secours in Lachine for a final blessing from the priest. We pay homage to Ronald, buying the customary quarter-pounder with cheese, Coke and French fries. We can't finish our meal, so we leave a few fries on top of a garbage can in the parking lot as an offering to the acolyte gulls that wait to receive them. But this is Yellowknife, not Toronto. Before the seabirds can make a move, a large, black raven swoops down from a gnarled spruce and eats its fill, the gulls forming a respectful semi-circle at a safe distance. Northern portent or not, this first wildlife observation of the expedition is faithfully recorded.

The few remaining errands in town completed, our mood of chatty excitement grows as we ride in Chris' battered, black Isuzu Trooper to a lakeside hangar owned by Air Tindi. They're one of the busiest air charter outfits in the Territories, and God willing, they will provide our ride back to Yellowknife at the end of August. We've arranged to leave the Trooper and our re-entry kits (clean clothes, keys, wallets, etc.) with Air Tindi and launch our watery adventure from the adjacent floatplane docks.

While we're off-loading the gear and our two 18½-foot Wenonah Kevlar canoes, Chris spies a pilot who had expressed doubts about Chris' initial tundra expedition last year. The reason for the scepticism was the unproven ability of a lightweight, Kevlar river runner to survive the rigours of a summer-long trip through the barrens. As it turned out, Chris and paddling partner Myrna were successful in their attempt, paddling from Fletcher Lake on the Hoarfrost River to Baker Lake via the Back and Thelon Rivers. They travelled in a Wenonah Odyssey, the same canoe Jill and I will use this year.

"I'm back!" taunts Chris, "and this time I've brought another one!" gesturing to the newer Minnesota II he and Christy will use. The former sceptic smiles, but remains silent. "You can't scare me this time!" Chris continues, as we pile our luggage at the shoreline and begin to get things sorted out. Any attempt at a reply is drowned out by the roar of a Twin Otter, taxiing up to the dock on its massive floats. The brief northern summer has begun, and Air Tindi's Yellowknife operation is going full bore. Barrels of fuel, bundles of geological equipment, boxes of core samples, and small clusters of people in various states of deportment and demeanour are continuously collected and deposited by an industrious fleet of white, float-equipped Cessnas and de Havilland Otters, each bearing the red Air Tindi logo.

With Great Slave Lake lapping at our boot tips after months of anticipation, we're anxious to begin, even though it's now late in the day. Our eagerness is tempered by a resolve to avoid dropping baggage into the lake, tripping over paddles, or otherwise malfunctioning in front of so many knowledgeable observers. We force ourselves to sort and load our gear slowly and methodically.

Once most other preparations are finished, there remains a final task: placing a few last-minute, long-distance telephone calls to impart farewells to distant family and friends. The bathroom in Air Tindi's hangar is another important last chance, and we each try to take advantage. In this, we're hampered by several intermittent power failures, which Air Tindi staff assure us are "par for the course for Yellowknife." One blackout occurs while I'm deep in the furthest recesses of the windowless washroom. After completing the necessary functions by touch and sound, the first navigational challenge of the summer is to work my way to the door and find the handle. This is accomplished without having to call for help.

At 7 p.m., all final arrangements satisfactorily completed, we slide ourselves into the boats, wriggle our bums to a comfortable operating position, hoist our paddles, and plunge them into the surface of the cold lake. Pulling away from Air Tindi's Lathem Island docks, we head southward, down Yellowknife Bay towards the open water and the distant horizon, dodging taxiing aircraft as we go.

Perhaps now is a good time to describe the members of our little gang of escapees. I'll start with our leader, Chris: twenty-seven years old, six feet, two inches tall, with blue eyes and light brown hair, shorn close to the scalp in preparation for the journey. He is a veteran of many long-haul canoe trips and has worked as a guide with Algonquin Outfitters in Ontario. I first met Chris through mutual friends who suggested me as a replacement for someone who backed out of a trip down the remote Nahanni River two years ago. I joined a party of five others led by Chris, and had an enjoyable, 14-day wilderness excursion. The trip was well-planned, well-provisioned and reasonably priced, factors I considered while deciding whether to take part in this current, more ambitious project.

Chris is a philosophy major, bound in the fall for a PhD program at Cambridge University. The son of a missionary, he was born in India. He received a large part of his early education at an American-run boarding school in Pakistan, where, by all accounts, he was the personification of a teacher's worst nightmare. One of the most striking facets of our leader is his unrestrained personality, felt as either silk or sandpaper, depending on the recipient's perspective and Chris's mood. Let me explain. Chris possesses a large, opinionated ego that irritates some, amuses others, and inspires still others to expand their own, more limited view of themselves. People in this latter category, encountering Chris in his full glory, ask themselves, "Why can't I be a little more like that?" Other observers, distracted and annoyed by his blunt comments and lack of humility, are less impressed. One of Chris' favourite poses, assumed when his navigational skills have been once again proven accurate, or when he has led his companions to a particularly scenic location, or has accomplished some other self-identified, praiseworthy feat, is the "Worship me!" position. On the Nahanni, this was executed either in the stern of his canoe or on some high place. He would stand, smiling broadly with arms upraised, palms up, invoking adulation. The flip side of these manifestations of conceit is his derogatory commentary on the words and actions of others. These unsolicited editorials are freely shared whenever his companions fail to meet his ever-changing but always demanding expectations, or when (for example) one of them buys a woman's golf hat.

If the above were the full width and breadth of Chris's personality, many more people would find him insufferable. As previously suggested, however, there's sometimes silk among the grit. Despite his attempts to pretend he's entirely without compassion ("It's hard for me to show how much I care, because I don't"), he is, in my estimation, genuinely concerned about the safety and comfort of those under his care. He often cooks the meals and eats only after everyone else has been served. He's generous with his personal possessions, frequently lending them out and sometimes not getting them back. While remaining blind to his own limitations, his self-confessed, youthful impatience with the foibles and anxieties of others has begun to mutate into a more laid-back and helpful attitude. A well-developed, if sometimes crude, sense of humour is ever-present, cushioning the difficulties and discomforts of life and travel in the wilderness. As far as blunt comments are concerned, he can take them as well as dish them out, which is unusual in the many big egos I've encountered in my 38 years. Most importantly for a trip of this duration, he is a skilled outdoorsman, thorough and meticulous to the smallest detail, which is probably the main reason I'm sitting in a narrow, yellow canoe, carving the smooth surface of Yellowknife Bay on a northern summer evening.

Chris's paddling partner Christy is in her mid-20s, five feet, four inches tall, with blue eyes and a boyish haircut, minimizing the need for maintenance *en route*. No doubt Chris will remedy her lack of paddling experience in his usual, subtle way. If she retains her sense of humour, Christy will learn a lot about canoeing and human nature. Like Chris, she's bound for doctoral studies in philosophy, in her case at Dalhousie University in Halifax. Apparently, they met at some philosophers' social event, although the details are sketchy. Unlike her paddling partner, Christy keeps her sandpaper out of sight and so far has been quiet and considerate. She's intelligent, but not of the forceful or opinionated variety. Christy's father is a university professor turned dairy farmer in Vankleek Hill near Ottawa. Years of daily chores down on the farm have instilled in her a mental and physical discipline that will be valuable in the days and weeks ahead. Whatever lies below the surface remains to be seen.

My paddling partner Jill is a friend of mine. We met a few years ago when the company I work for sent me on a brief assignment to our nation's capital. I won't mention her age except to say it matches mine (see above). Our junior travelling companions playfully refer to us as the geriatric canoe. I smile and reflect that it's a pleasure to experience an inter-generational activity, so rare in chronologically compartmentalized North American culture. We trust that our youthful companions will benefit from the 76 years of accumulated wisdom in the adjacent canoe. But I digress. Jill has brown eyes and has also cropped her formerly long, brown hair, one of several sacrifices for the sake of the trip. A nurse in Ottawa, she holds down two jobs, apparently with two very understanding employers. Canoeing, winter camping and hiking have long been her passions. As a measure of her commitment, she owns two canoes and has accumulated such a variety of outdoor equipment that she's known to her friends as "Mountain Jill." Her canoeing experience far exceeds mine, so she'll command the stern of our boat. Judging by the way she handled the packs on the dock, she'll do more than her share of the grunt work without hesitation or complaint. When I told her about this trip, she joined up with such enthusiasm that my lingering doubts were swept aside and I finalized my own decision to go.

As for me, much of who I am will probably leak from between the lines of this journal. Here's a bit more. I work at a consulting engineering company near Toronto, where I help clients navigate the bureaucracy that stands between what we in the business call "raw land" and "development": those seemingly endless acres of houses, parking lots and shopping malls that surround our major cities. A loyal, hardworking employee of the firm for the past 14 years, I've decided to cash in some of this accumulated goodwill in the form of a two-month leave of absence (unpaid, of course).

My outdoor passion began during a co-op work term at the University of Waterloo, when I was sent to northern Manitoba to live in a tent for the winter. Along with learning how to cut firewood with a bucksaw, chop water holes in frozen lakes, and use snowshoes, I operated electromagnetic survey equipment as part of an exploration program for base metals (copper, zinc, and lead). I occasionally camp, hike, and cross-country ski, but have limited canoeing experience. Apart from a few short, flat-water day trips, I spent one weekend on the whitewater of the Magnetawan River in Ontario (where I swamped, but did not sink), and those two weeks on the Nahanni, where I benefited from my stern-person's experience and came through dry as a bone. While others my age have sought adventure through marriages, children, mortgages or divorce, I've not yet been challenged in any of these areas. I'm therefore left to seek stimulation by other means.

Having described the cast of characters, I now return to our expedition, already in progress.

The weather on our departure is calm and overcast with light westerly winds and gentle swell. These pick up as we move further down the bay. We're dive-bombed by the occasional, anxious gull or tern as we pass too near their nesting sites on the many rocky shoals that dot the undulating, grey water. We also notice clusters of floating loons. They're much friendlier than their southern cousins, allowing us to get within a few metres before diving.

We arrive at our island camp at 9:25 p.m., having made a distance of 12 kilometres. The bugs (mosquitoes) at this place are denser and more persistent than expected, given the brisk wind and exposed location. I've already been roundly "mosquitoed" and look forward to a time in the not-too-distant future when my beard has grown thick enough to provide added protection. These early attacks may be a grim foreshadowing of what we'll experience on the barrens.

Apart from the insects, our island is a pleasant refuge, reminiscent of parts of Georgian Bay or the Nova Scotia seacoast near Halifax, according to Christy. Group-of-Seven type scenery surrounds us: open sky, rippled water, sculpted granite, and contorted spruce. This island is one of thousands lining both sides of Yellowknife Bay, creating a labyrinth of scenic, sheltered passages for canoeing. The pink and grey rocks along the waterline are bedecked with the distinctive, orange starburst pattern of jewel lichen, fertilized, our field guide says, by bird droppings. Makes sense. And so...to bed. After this hectic day, an early night is appreciated by all.

Camp Location: 62° 22.55'N 114° 17.85'W
Distance Today: 12 km. paddle, 0 km. portage
Distance to Date: 12 km. paddle, 0 km. portage

July 3 and 4

Editor's Note: Journal entries for the 3rd and 4th of July are missing from the narrative. Based on a review of contemporary sources, this is attributed to the author suffering from a noxious combination of fatigue, sore muscles, and general disorientation. Distances travelled and camp locations are provided below:

Camp Location (July 3): 62° 07.50'N 113° 47.70'W
Distance Today: 44 km. paddle, 0 km. portage
Distance to Date: 56 km. paddle, 0 km. portage

Camp Location (July 4): 61° 59.50'N 113° 14.75'W
Distance Today: 35 km. paddle, 0 km. portage
Distance to Date: 91 km. paddle, 0 km. portage

July 5

We're sheltering in a small cove west of the Francois River, held up by wind, rain and heavy swell after fighting these conditions for a couple of hours and landing here for a rest. Already, we've experienced many of the lake's moods, ranging from bucolic sunshine with flat calm to dangerous waves driven by stiff, cold wind.

July 3rd is a barely remembered blur of effort, but I'm able to recount some of what happened yesterday. We passed through Devil's Channel, northwest of the Caribou Islands. This sheltered, inside passage about seven kilometres in length let us avoid the more exposed, western end of Hearne Channel. We enjoyed this convenient bypass and saw no apparent reason for its formidable name. There's a large navigational beacon at the channel's west end, along with a Canadian Coast Guard compound containing fuel drums, buoys and anchors. A small cemetery is located near the east end, south of Goulet Bay. We landed there briefly to explore, but were dissuaded by swarms of large, persistent horseflies.

When we reached the mouth of Campbell Bay, Chris began trolling from the stern of his canoe using a rod, reel, and durable 30-pound test line. These were given to him by a group of airborne fishermen from Portland, Oregon, whom Chris and Myrna encountered during last year's tundra trip. Besides giving them fishing tackle and cold beer, the group invited them into one of their two vintage, 1939 Grumman Goose amphibious aircraft. Once aboard, they were able to phone home via shortwave radio with the help of a marine operator in San Francisco. The group also taught Chris and Myrna how to fillet their catches. Teach a man to fish and you feed him for a lifetime, or at least until he finishes his canoe trip. Using their newly acquired skills and equipment, the latter replacing a rod lost in an earlier mishap, Chris and Myrna were able to augment their daily rations with regular infusions of fresh protein. This year, we all hope to be beneficiaries; within a few minutes of dropping a line into the lake, Chris hooked a five-pound lake trout. Not enough meat on him to make a full meal, but he (actually, she, judging by the roe) made a welcome addition to last night's dinner menu. From lake to pan in about two hours...fine for us, but probably disorienting for the fish.

As for today's effort, so far it's been a hard, windy slog along a very small portion of a very large lake. Conditions are unchanged as of 5 p.m., so we decide to stay where we are for the night. The distance will have to be made up later, but there's no sense in struggling along the smooth-sided north shore of Hearne Channel with conditions as they are.

I climb a small, rocky knoll east of camp with our electronic wind gauge. Hoisting it aloft and pushing the button, I get a peak reading of about 35 kilometres per hour. Not much of a gale, but paddling into it head-on is hard work. The swell we encountered during today's brief effort averaged about three feet, with an occasional bit of surprising, four-foot chop. Such waves are disconcerting when experienced in a narrow, pitching canoe in cold, deep water. I've not paddled in such conditions on a lake before. This can't accurately be called flatwater canoeing. Our heavily loaded boats rode the waves surprisingly well, hulls rising on each successive crest, and then pitching downwards, slapping the water with a hollow, jarring "boom." I got quite wet in the bouncy bow. The Velcro fasteners on the spray skirt's cockpit openings could do with a bit of redesigning, I think. Fortunately, the nylon river pants we all picked up at Mountain Equipment Co-op are quick to dry. We've found that it's best to leave our wet clothing on and let our surplus body heat speed the drying process. It's either that, or switch to Gore-Tex, which is a bit too hot and heavy for current temperatures.

While considering the implications of the wind and waves for our safety, I recall something Guy Blanchet learned while making a survey for the Canadian government in 1924. As he crossed Great Slave Lake by canoe in a heavy swell, his Chipewyan assistants, Basile and Sousi, described a traditional tactic for coping with such conditions: *"If the canoes were heavy laden, first the women were thrown overboard, then the dogs."* To show there was no inequality, Sousi assured Blanchet that *"...sometimes even the men would drown."* This Aboriginal tradition doesn't translate well to our current situation. We have no dogs, and without Jill at the rudder (assuming I could somehow get her out of the boat), I would drown that much faster.

Our course of the past few days is the reverse of that taken by Alexander Mackenzie in June of 1789, as he paddled westward on his way to descend the 1700-kilometre-long river that would eventually bear his name. This roving trader-explorer completed his journey from Lake Athabasca to the Arctic Ocean in about 40 days, moving as one historian has noted *"...like a latter-day Cortez, conquering the land with his Scot's acumen and his formidable prose."* Mackenzie was hoping to reach the Pacific. I'll bet his prose was especially formidable once he realized he was at the wrong ocean.

Today's high temperature was about 60°F, but even with the brisk headwind, it was still possible to work up a good sweat with the paddle. Yesterday's bright sun and mid-70s temperatures had us all in our shirt sleeves. So far, water temperatures have ranged from a high of about 58°F along the margins of Yellowknife Bay to a chilly 42°F beside our current camp.

The friendliness of the loons populating this vast lake continues to this day. They appear almost glad to see us. A flotilla of six enters our small cove this evening, coming to within a few metres of shore and giving us the eye before commencing their usual bobbing and diving. Spruce and balsam poplars grow here in profusion along the rocky, windswept headlands, while verdant wetlands line the sheltered coves. This is quintessential, boreal canoe country, magnified in our imaginations by the immense size of Great Slave Lake and the bold ambition of our summer's work. We're still 250 kilometres from lake's end, and that's just the starting line for our journey.

Camp Location: 62° 0.95' N 113° 05.18' W
Distance Today: 9 km. paddle, 0 km. portage
Distance to Date: 100 km. paddle, 0 km. portage

Chapter 2: DIARRHEA! DIARRHEA!

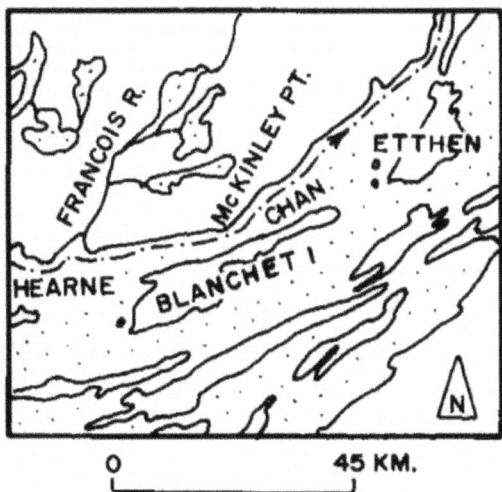

July 6

    We arrived at a small cove just west of McKinley Point at 6:30 p.m. after 10½ hours spent battling the northeast winds and swell that have become the norm. Like yesterday, the canoes bucked high on each successive wave crest and crashed heavily downward into the intervening troughs. I'm sure it was only adrenaline and hard work that kept me from getting seasick. Jill and I were bow-heavy today due to our baggage placement. We paid for this by taking on several gallons of water while fighting our way northeast to reach the lee of some islands in Francois Bay. Despite the spray skirt, we had to pause to bail, fearing that the water leaking into the cockpit openings and sloshing back and forth in the canoe bottom would overturn us.

    As of 10 p.m., the wind is gone, and the persistent cloud cover of the past two days has broken, so we expect fine paddling weather tomorrow. It's 60°F this evening while the water temperature in our little cove sits at 48°F. No one is swimming.

I make this entry lying on smooth, flat bedrock, protected from the marauding insects by a bug shirt, which, with its light-coloured cotton body and full-face mask, resembles a fencing uniform. It's satisfying to wear something so simple yet so effective in thwarting the designs of the carnivorous, airborne hordes. I wore it during our after-dinner tea, and the mask is now stained brown where I sipped the hot drink directly through the mesh. This strategy not only kept the bugs at bay, but it also strained the inevitable floaters out of the brew. Besides this defensive shield, we're protected this evening by a symbiosis of a sort; just as we attract clouds of whining mosquitoes, these attract squadrons of dragonflies, darting and buzzing like Battle of Britain Spitfires as they snatch and devour mosquitoes in mid-flight. It's nice to have a miniature air force on our side for a change.

Camp is made, and dinner is done. We putter about at various, minor chores, illuminated by persistent daylight. Chris is casting his line from the shore, using a second, lighter rod and reel in hopes of repeating his earlier success. Jill and Christy reorganize the food and sort out the various cooking utensils in the square wooden box called a wanigan, the heart of our outdoor kitchen. The tents are pitched on gently rounded mounds of pink, lichen-stained granite. A silent line of white spruce, illuminated by the low-angled sun, crowns the ridge across the cove from our camp. It's a pleasant setting, ideal for rest and deep reflection, but most of us are still too wound up for that.

Tonight, we amuse ourselves with a few rounds of competitive, extemporaneous poetry. Christy (who apparently believes that art should imitate life) decides that the topic should be diarrhea. The idea is to create a metaphorical description, a rhyming couplet in the style of William Shakespeare or maybe Noël Coward. I can't resist documenting a few of the submissions:

When you thought that you were Prussian,

Diarrhea! Diarrhea!

But it turns out you're a Russian:
Diarrhea!
Diarrhea!

When you'd gladly trade your best date,
For a jar of Kaopectate:
Diarrhea!
Diarrhea!

Editor's Note: The narrative continues in graphic detail.
Portions have been deleted.

Camp Location: 62° 04.60'N 112° 28.52'W
Distance Today: 35 km. paddle, 0 km. portage
Distance to Date: 135 km. paddle, 0 km. portage

July 7

My paddle's keen and bright...NOT! For one thing, it's not my paddle. It belongs to Myrna, Chris's paddling partner from last year. I do own one; it's safely attached to the canoe by Velcro loops and a pocket sewn into the spray skirt. It'll stay there unless needed as an emergency replacement. Myrna's paddle was slated to fill that backup role, but just before heading out from the Air Tindi docks, I hefted this spare blade and discovered that it was about two inches shorter than my own. It was therefore easier to wield. Just as in those far-off days when I played floor hockey every Tuesday night down at Knox Presbyterian Church in Toronto, I'm finding that a shorter stick works better for me. I prefer to trade off some reach for a greater degree of control. This may be a character revelation, or it may simply have something to do with the length of my arms.

Also, my paddle isn't bright. It's a jet-black Barton blade, woven from carbon fibres like each of the others. Light and strong, it has no flexibility or springiness. That means most of the backward thrust put into it by the paddler translates into forward motion of the boat. High school physics is a big part of canoeing, it seems. Since the motive force is drawn from our muscles via the food in our stomachs, and our food is of finite quantity, energy efficiency is critical. The paddle shaft is bent at an angle just above the blade (I'm told it's 14 degrees, but I have no way to confirm it). This increases the effective length of the power portion of the stroke. Our paddles weigh little, so we use them at what seems to me a fast cadence for an 8-week marathon. We reach forward and plant our shafts vertically into the water and then pull ourselves towards them with our shoulders, thighs and stomachs, slicing the blade sideways, out of the water when they're opposite our hips. When there's a headwind, we feather our paddles as we swing them forward, turning the blade horizontal to the water to reduce air resistance. We paddle in sync, bow and stern blades entering the water simultaneously (more or less). The person in the stern, when so inclined, calls out, "Switch!" and both paddlers simultaneously switch sides, ideally without missing a stroke. In theory, this paddling style will allow the canoes to hold their course and maintain their momentum: more high school physics at work.

So then, what about the canoes? Well, as mentioned earlier, we're using 18½-foot Kevlar boats. Descendants of earlier designs with a river racing pedigree, they were built by the Wenonah Company of Minnesota. They're light (about 55 pounds) and pointed at the ends, giving them an elongated diamond shape when viewed from above. My boat felt tippy at first, according to my limited paddling experience, but both craft seem at home in the heavy swell we've paddled through so far. I have a feeling it would take a lot to knock them over. Built with a long, flat keel, they track well, i.e., they tend to maintain their direction. That means they require more effort to turn than a shorter boat or one with more "rocker" (upturned ends). We sit on comfortable bucket seats that Chris has padded with blue polyethylene foam. These are low-slung, so kneeling is out of the question, no matter how lumpy the water. We sit with legs stretched out in front, kayak style, or wedged into whatever position the baggage allows. Generous foam thigh braces help us maintain an efficient operating position. Chris and Christy paddle a new Minnesota II (M2); Jill and I use an Odyssey, already careworn from its previous trip to the barrens and an ice-bashing, early spring trip in Algonquin Park a few months ago.

Both boats are fitted with removable spray skirts: fabric decking designed to help keep the cargo in and the water out. The M2's skirt is a three-piece setup (front, middle and back), attached to the gunnels by a wide strip of Velcro. The skirt on the Odyssey is a one-piece, all-or-nothing, lace-up version held in place by thin rope threaded through small loops fixed to the sides of the boat. It's more tedious to operate, but when properly attached, it seems less likely to peel off when the going gets rough.

So why take such canoes to the subarctic? As I understand it, as explained by Chris, it's because of the long distances and the heavy loads our journey entails. Using our selected combination of paddle and canoe, even boats with rookies in the bow can cruise along comfortably at about six to seven kilometres per hour, roughly the pace of a brisk walk. Shorter Royalex canoes, arguably more rugged and manoeuvrable, can't match this pace for hours at a time, day after day, without the paddlers working a lot harder, and they don't have the baggage capacity we need. Mostly, we'll be travelling on lakes rather than winding streams or rocky rapids, so our Wenonahs should do the trick. Their practicality for northern exposure was demonstrated by Chris and Myrna last summer, as well as by a few others previously, so we boldly go.

Our choice of canoes will probably have other implications, which I intend to record as I become aware of them. The first thing I notice is that our vehicles are essentially just thin, translucent shells of fabric and resin. When the sun shines on the hull, and the spray skirt is open, it's easy to see the waterline from the inside. While disconcerting at first, it's handy for loading up, since it's easy to tell if the canoe is leaning to the left or right. This must be corrected to avoid a sore back after a long day of paddling. A well-balanced load also ensures that the canoe doesn't develop a tendency to veer off course, and most importantly, it helps keep the whole thing from going bottom-up in rough water. As for the long axis, we've found that our boats are most manoeuvrable and least prone to swamping when more of the weight is towards the stern. Because of this and because the canoes are narrow at either end, baggage must be placed with care and forethought. No hasty dumping it in at the last minute, even when the insects are swarming and the other boat is hovering impatiently offshore.

After this lengthy digression (I'm easily distracted), I return my attention to our journey. It's a beautiful day of mirror-calm water and warm sunshine. We take full advantage of the amiable conditions and put 48 kilometres between us and our last camp. This is accomplished in consecutive paddling sessions of three, three, and two hours, with breaks of about an hour in between, a working day of about 10 hours all told.

Jill and I are generally quiet as we paddle. Jill sometimes hums or sings softly, while I have frequent out-of-body experiences, lulled by the paddling routine. One of my amusements is to transport myself to "Sam the Record Man" on Yonge Street in Toronto, where I browse vicariously through the classical music department searching for appealing CDs to add to my modest collection. Today, I imagine that I've located a hard-to-find disc by the Drakensberg Boys' Choir of Natal, South Africa and congratulate myself on my good fortune, and then Jill calls out, "Switch!" and I'm pulled back to Great Slave Lake. Chris and Christy often engage in lengthy, intense discussions encompassing a variety of scholarly topics. The canoes are generally too far apart for Jill and me to listen in, but when the wind is low, we can sometimes hear snippets of a wide-ranging, philosophical debate wafting across the calm, cold water. Today's topic seems to be radical feminism or something in a similar vein. I much prefer a quiet boat.

Diarrhea! Diarrhea!

This evening we're camped in a slight indentation in the north shore of the lake, opposite the cliffs of Etthen Island. In September of 1890, the British adventurer Warburton Pike made his first north shore landfall at a cove just east of here, while on his way north to explore and hunt musk oxen. He noted in his journal that Et-then means "the Caribou" in the Chipewyan [Ojibwe] language. He also remarked on the cliffs of Etthen Island, describing them as *"...remarkable many coloured bluff[s] composed of soft rock used by the Indians for the manufacture of their stone pipes."* This evening, they are indeed multi-coloured and beautiful as the sun strikes them at a low angle, illuminating horizontal bands of pink, mauve, and grey.

It's disorienting for southerners to find ourselves living under a sun that circles the horizon instead of rising and setting in the familiar cycle of the lower latitudes. According to our GPS, the sun will set at 11:16 this evening and rise again at 3:48 a.m. Even when the sun is down, the sky remains bright with twilight.

Camp Location: 62° 21.27'N 111° 49.67'W
Distance Today: 48 km. paddle, 0 km. portage
Distance to Date: 183 km. paddle, 0 km. portage

Chapter 3: ICE PANS AND SNOWDRIFT

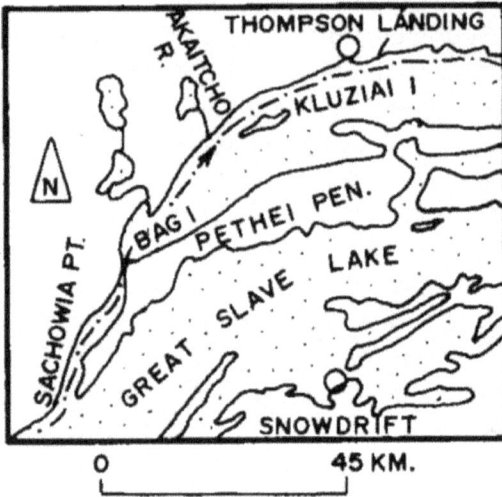

July 8

We make about 50 kilometres today, aided by a brisk tailwind. Tonight's island camp has many natural amenities, including a small bathing pool of sun-warmed water trapped in a pocket of smooth bedrock. Pleasing scenery abounds, and insects are few. We scamper about, barefoot on the warm granite. There's something special about camping on islands. Maybe it's the sense of isolation and security they afford, or perhaps just the aesthetic synergy of rock, tree, sky and water. The hunter-explorer David T. Hanbury recalled of his own passage of Great Slave Lake in 1899: "*...lonely yet indescribably friendly, every moss-clad island seemed to invite us to camp there, offering deeper and softer moss, whiter birch-bark trees, more sheltering pines and firs, sweeter balsam boughs.*"

Today's route takes us around Sachowia Point, north of the Pethei Peninsula and its steep, north-facing cliffs. All remains as described by Lieutenant George Back of the Royal Navy on August 14th, 1833, while on an expedition that over two years would take him to the Arctic Ocean via the Great Fish River. Like Alexander Mackenzie, Back ended up having a river named after him; future cartographers crossed out "Great Fish" and inserted "Back." Unlike Mackenzie, Back wanted to go north. His mission was to lay the geographical groundwork for Sir John Franklin's ongoing quest for the Northwest Passage. I can't improve on the flowery prose of this sailor-artist, who described the Pethei as *"...one uninterrupted mural precipice, along the base of which* [is] *a succession of trap hills with similar faces and rounded summits."* We find, as Back did, that the north-facing edge of the Pethei doesn't offer much in the way of campsites. Like him, we choose to stay close to the northern shore *"...on the declivities of which some patches of last winter's snow were yet visible."* Today, fortunately, all visible declivities are snow-free.

Ok. It's time to confess that over the winter months, I spent many happy hours sifting through historical journals and annotating the margins of my 1:250,000 scale maps with pithy, geographically appropriate quotes for casual insertion into my own chronicle. I also hope to spice up my casual dinner conversation and counterbalance the intellectual weight of the philosophers. So far, this conversational gambit seems to be working. I just have to be careful to memorize my lines. Reading quotes from a map wouldn't have the desired effect.

In the afternoon, we paddle through Taltheilei Narrows and approach Plummer's fishing lodge. It's a substantial operation, with various outbuildings, radio masts, docks, a marina and a gravel airstrip. The American flag is prominently displayed, indicating the origin of most of the clients. As we near the main lodge, our canoes begin to buck in the wash kicked up by a fleet of powerboats churning to and fro, ferrying wealthy anglers to their dream fishing holes. We have no worries in this regard because Chris is already trolling and soon comes through with an extremely large lake trout, whose weight we conservatively estimate at about 20 pounds. When our fish strikes at the lure, Chris drops his paddle, grabs the rod, and pulls hard to set the hook. His canoe stops abruptly, appearing to move backwards through the water as Christy rests on her paddle and Jill and I coast by, already starting to salivate. After letting the monster exhaust itself in a tug of war with the boat, Chris hauls it in, and with Christy's help, levers it into the canoe with a dip net.

Most of the fishermen in the passing powerboats ignore us, intent on landing the big one themselves, before they're compelled to leave again for the south. It's hard to blame them. The meter is running, and here, just as back at the office, time costs money. Never happy when ignored, Chris decides to goad them a bit with his latest catch. As the next boat approaches, Chris grins widely and stands up, balancing himself in the stern of the canoe as he hoists the trout aloft. Its tail is almost touching the bottom of the canoe while the head is level with his waist. The fishermen swivel their heads in our direction and eye this glistening, silver trophy. Their boat slows, and a grudging, "Nice fish," floats across the water above the muted grumbling of the outboard. Chris continues to pose, still grinning as the rest of us snap pictures of our next meal. It's a classic example of the "Worship me!" pose, except that Chris's hands are full, so he can't raise his arms in victory. We willingly grant him this moment; by filling our stomachs, he's earned our praise. After landing on the nearby shore, he carves out several huge, boneless fillets, leaving the guts, spine, head and tail for a circle of admiring gulls anxiously awaiting our departure.

East of the narrows, we pass down the north side of Bag Island. Chief Factor Anderson and his assistant, James Stewart of the Hudson Bay Company, camped here during an expedition mounted in 1855, in a belated, unsuccessful search for the long-dead John Franklin and party. During the 1940s, the full text of Anderson's journal was published in serial form in the Canadian Field Naturalist. I'm indebted to Bill, a companion from the Nahanni trip, for providing me with copies. The most revealing entry was penned at the end of the journey. After weeks of detached prose, recording in a matter-of-fact style the feats they accomplished and hardships they shared, the lid came off and Anderson exploded that Stewart *"...was perfectly useless to me and nothing more than a mere encumbrance."* It's a performance evaluation unlikely to lead to promotion. I hope my companions on this present enterprise will speak better of me than that, once our travel is done. Then again, I hold the pen for this expedition's journal, so I shouldn't fare too badly.

During his stop, Anderson noted the presence of eagles' nests at Bag Island, and we're able to confirm that their descendants continue to nest here, 140 years later. We pass close to the island's north side and see one at the top of a dead tree near the water's edge, guarding a nest. Camera shutters click as the big bird glowers fiercely from its lofty perch, and a second eagle soars watchfully overhead. No one climbs the tree to look for eggs. At the east end of this same island, rugged, 400-foot cliffs rise vertically from the water.

Today's air temperature reached the low 60s F, but as of 10 p.m., it has cooled off considerably. Time to turn in. The bugs have descended in force, and wake-up has been set for 7 a.m. We hope to make another 50 kilometres tomorrow, God and the weather permitting, and we aim to reach Pike's portage at the east end of the lake in about four more days.

Camp Location: 62° 43.80'N 111° 20.87'W
Distance Today: 50 km. paddle, 0 km. portage
Distance to Date: 233 km. paddle, 0 km. portage

July 9

We paddle 47 kilometres today and make our camp on a small point near the mouth of the Waldron River. It's another superb setting, similar to last night's stop. Tents are pitched on smooth, bare rock, and a light breeze keeps the insects at bay. The final rapids of the steeply descending stream are hidden from view, but their roar is audible through the trees.

Bathed in bright sunlight, the water was calm throughout today's passage, with only a gentle headwind to dapple the surface. We've noticed that the breezes on this large lake have a peculiar habit of changing their temperature while maintaining their direction. When the wind turns cold, we pull on our fleece jackets. When it warms up, we take them off again. We make this switch four or five times during a typical day. Sometimes, a thin layer of mist forms above the sparkling water as the lake chills a migrating pocket of warm, moist air. Though we sometimes get sweaty while paddling, it's impossible to forget we're on a northern lake. Stray droplets of water from carelessly swung paddles strike warm arms and faces like icy bullets. Near the mouth of the Akaitcho River, a cluster of last winter's ice pans lies grounded in a small bay, evidence of the dominance of the subarctic's longest season.

We pass a couple of kilometres south of Thompson Landing and notice several buildings, but no boats or other signs of life. We also cross the mouth of the Mountain River. Here, Warburton Pike left the lake and headed north to the tundra in search of musk oxen. Based on descriptions provided him by others, he had assumed these would be a ferocious and elusive quarry, a test of his skill and bravery. Ultimately, he was disappointed if not embarrassed by the ease with which these large creatures could be dispatched with a single, well-aimed bullet as they stood in an outward-facing circle, protecting their young.

As he passed along the north shore, Pike noticed, as we do, that "...countless streams, the outlets of lakes on the elevated tableland to the north, *foam down the deep gulches in the hillsides...*" We hear several of these torrents and see one stream that has remained frozen and clings, glacier-like, to rocks high above Great Slave. In the foreground, stunted spruce trees coat the rocky shoreline in ragged patches of subdued green, punctuated by knobs of naked rock, 500 to 600 feet high. Somewhere over this grim, northern horizon, patrolled by mosquitoes, black flies and ravens, lies the fabled barren lands which we hope to enter via Artillery Lake in about a week's time. As the sun continues to beat down on the exposed coast, banks of white, cumulus clouds form above the land, buoyed by thermals rising from the sun-warmed rock. The cooler, denser air above the water remains a profound cloudless blue. The demarcation between white and blue paints a life-sized map of the coastline in the sky above, showing us the way forward.

We're starting to feel more isolated out here towards the lake's east end. To the best of our knowledge, the nearest permanent settlement is Snowdrift, about 60 kilometres away on the south shore. One sign of civilization that we notice is a navigational beacon on a small island east of the mouth of the Mountain River.

There's been discussion within our small group about the relative merits of wearing a lifejacket for 10 hours a day. It's the old comfort versus caution debate that arises in all manner of human activity. Chris doesn't wear one, cheerfully predicting that in the event of an upset, hypothermia will quickly kill us, floatation or no. I'm firmly on the "pro jacket" side of the debate, but I'm alone; the women choose to wear theirs only when they think conditions warrant. I'm so dogmatic in my argument that Chris reacts by posting a sarcastic, $10 reward for anyone who obtains a photograph of me in the canoe without my life jacket. It's ironic because he sold me the jacket this spring, telling me how comfortable it would be for daily use. I make a counter-proposal: if no one manages to get the photograph over the course of the summer, each of the others must pay me $10. They respond with a promise to buy me a steak dinner at the Wildcat Café in Yellowknife if the photo isn't obtained. It's a good deal for me, since there's no way I'll be out of pocket. I'm already counting on that dinner and trying to decide what I'll order for dessert. Today, it would be a thick wedge of warm cherry pie with vanilla ice cream.

The spectacular cliffs along the north shore of the Kahochella Peninsula are visible 12 kilometres south of camp, across McLeod Bay. Our maps show that some of these tower 700 feet above the lake. Had it not been our plan to visit an isolated homestead at the mouth of the Hoarfrost River in a couple of days, we might have chosen to cross McLeod Bay in the lee of Kluziai Island to get a closer look.

The air temperature remained in the low to mid 60s F today. A measurement taken while Chris was landing another lake trout showed a water temperature of 48 °. The bright sun and reflective water have taken their toll; we were all a little burnt today, where sunscreen was carelessly applied.

Camp Location: 62° 55.87'N 110° 34.66'W
Distance Today: 47 km. paddle, 0 km. portage
Distance to Date: 280 km. paddle, 0 km. portage

Christy and Chris enjoy an unusually calm day on Great Slave Lake.

Jill and I prepare to depart a buggy campsite (Chris Morris).

An island camp on Great Slave Lake.

One of the many lake trout that didn't get away.

Chapter 4: HOARFROST, HUSKIES AND MEN FROM MASSACHUSETTS

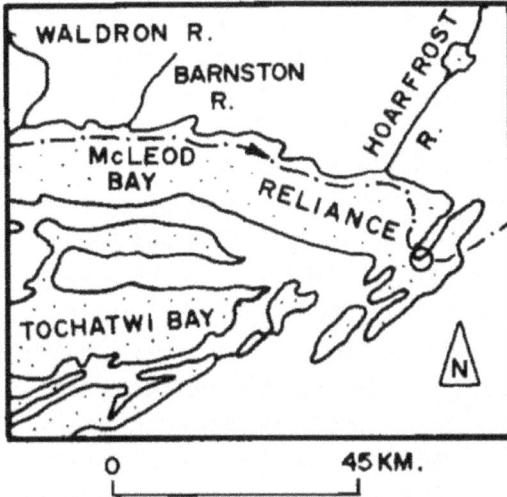

July 10

    This morning, we make a brief stop below a waterfall at the mouth of the Barnston River. Chris wants to try casting his line from the boat, a change in angling strategy from all the trolling he's done so far. While we loiter there in our canoes, a blue, single-engine Cessna floatplane appears overhead. After making a quick overflight, it circles round and then drops lightly onto the surface of the lake before taxiing over towards the falls. The engine stops, and two men climb down from the cramped cockpit onto the floats to stretch their legs. We paddle over to say hello. During our brief conversation, they tell us that they've flown all the way from Massachusetts to sample the local fishing. They're anxious to drop in a line, and soon retrieve their tackle from the back seat and begin casting. A few minutes later, when there are no bites or nibbles, they decide to troll. One man climbs back into the cockpit and starts the engine while the other switches lures. Soon, the aircraft is motoring back and forth in front of the falls, trailing a line: a noisy and expensive imitation of what we do with the canoes.

We decide to depart for quieter regions and head southeast towards the main body of the lake. On our way out of the small bay at the river mouth, both canoes narrowly avoid running up against a barely submerged rib of rock running parallel to the shore. A collision could have caused serious damage to our heavily loaded Kevlar envelopes, but we manage to put the brakes on in time. I now know how to back-paddle with a bent-shaft blade; it's exactly the same way as with a conventional one. I'm guessing this newly acquired skill will be of further use during our journey. As we continue eastward, we hear engine noise from behind as the Cessna takes to the skies once more. The boys from New England have also given up and are heading elsewhere. That's the way to fish up here. No need to be patient. If they aren't biting in one spot, there are lots of other places to try your luck. If you're mobile, just move on.

Tonight, we're holed up in a small cove three kilometres east of Big Stone Point, after fighting a strong headwind that began in the mid-afternoon. Our camp is near a former settlement once visited by Ernest Thompson Seton, a well-known author and naturalist of his day. In the spring of 1907, on his way to the barrens to study caribou, he stopped there to obtain provisions:

My crew seized their rifles to let [the] *Village know we were coming. The camp came quickly into view and volley after volley was fired and returned. These Indians are extremely poor and the shots cost 5-6¢ each. So this demonstration totalled up about $2... As soon as we were ashore, a number of Indians came to offer meat for tobacco... Food they could do without for a long time but life without smoke was intolerable; and they offered their whole dry product of 2 Caribou, concentrated nourishing food enough to last a family many days, in exchange for half a pound of stinking, nasty, poisonous tobacco.*

Camp Location: 62° 55.52'N 109° 54.95'W

Distance Today: 35 km. paddle, 0 km. portage
Distance to Date: 315 km. paddle, 0 km. portage

July 11

    We made 43 kilometres this day, which included a two-hour stop at Dave and Kristen's Hoarfrost River homestead. Dave is a bush pilot, and he and Kristen raise and race sled dogs. As we cross the bay at the mouth of the river and head towards the small cluster of buildings tucked into the northeast corner, I'm glad that it's not 1907. Even if we had the weapons, we'd be ill-advised to fire "volley after volley" from our lively Wenonahs; the recoil would soon have us swimming. In any event, it's not rifle fire that greets us, but the banshee yips and howls of 36 Huskies, each one tethered in front of its own home: an inverted oil drum with a door cut into the side. A sturdy, wire fence guards this dog city, while a separate, segregated compound holds a gaggle of pups.

    We're received by Megan, a friend of Dave and Kristen, who is staying with them for the summer. There's no need to knock. She meets us at the water, having had ample warning of our arrival. She tells us that her hosts have gone to Yellowknife in their aircraft. After looking us over briefly, she decides we're harmless and invites us up to her cabin for a visit.

    We learn that Megan has had a variety of northern experiences, including work in various geological camps, both as a cook and a geological assistant, operating a magnetometer. She says there's been a boom in exploration over the past several years, with diamonds the primary source of interest. She tells us it's possible to make good money in the camps, but for now she has all the cash she needs and is enjoying the solitude out here near the lake's remote east end. This winter, she'll migrate southwest to the mountain slopes of British Columbia, where she'll work as a ski instructor and guide.

    Megan serves up our first taste of northern hospitality, plying us with all the hot coffee and freshly baked cookies we can handle. She also gives us a tour of this impressive settlement. There are two log dwellings, with a third under construction. The latter has three storeys and a south-facing balcony. There's a sauna, and several sheds and outbuildings. And of course, there are the dogs. As we stand at the edge of Dog City, I'm reminded of the Bugs Bunny cartoon where the hungry cat, Sylvester, is separated from the delicious Tweety Bird by a yard filled with barking, prancing canines. Fortunately, the ones here are well-contained, and we have no cause to wade through them on stilts like the ill-fated Sylvester. Even so, Jill's shirt is torn by one animal wishing to say a special hello.

We return to Megan's cabin and write postcards (gloat cards?) to family and friends. Megan promises to mail them when the opportunity arises. Not wishing to wear out our welcome, we snatch a few more cookies, snap some pictures and then head back to the boats. Megan gives her address to Chris and asks to be informed if he's running another barrens trip next year. It seems he's won another convert.

This afternoon, we have our first heavy rain while paddling and have a chance to try out our waterproof coats. Mine is a rugged, Marmot-brand Gore-Tex jacket: a hand-me-down tundra veteran I bought from Chris. He now sports an attention-grabbing, yellow-orange, high-tech garment interwoven with strands of Kevlar. The women also have bright apparel. Jill's is a rich derivative of purple, while Christy is resplendent in red, with royal blue trim. Since my own jacket is a muted grey, I wear a bright orange toque to compensate. Add in the two flashy yellow canoes, and we make a fine display. Even the brilliant-hued birds of the rainforest would be jealous.

As I write this at our camp, several kilometres east of Dave and Kristen's homestead, the rain is abating and the sun is peeking through a thin veil of fog. The emerging sun and calm weather bode well for tomorrow's planned 12-kilometre crossing of McLeod Bay to Reliance. We hope to reach the lower end of Pike's Portage in the afternoon. We'll enjoy stretching our legs after cruising on this lake for the past nine days.

Due to the rain, our cooking shelter is erected for the first time this trip. It's a pyramid-shaped Black Diamond tent, pegged to the ground at all four corners and supported by a single, central pole. High enough to stand up in, it easily accommodates the four of us and our wanigan. Although it has no floor, this modern tepee keeps the wind and rain at bay. Once a mosquito coil is installed, the bugs cease to be a factor, except that they tend to rain down from the tent's peak into our food, once overcome by the fumes. Chris first tested this rig last year on the tundra and had it enlarged during the winter to accommodate our party of four.

Tonight's supper is pasta with dried beef, dried mushrooms, and onions. We each swallow a handful of M&M peanut candies for dessert. During an after-dinner stroll, I spy traces of an earlier camp, including rusted tin cans and rotted wood still stacked for burning. This isn't the first time we've found ourselves camped among the leavings of others. It's surprising to me how much of this lakeshore has been visited and used; or is it just that great minds think alike, and we've all tended to pick the same campsites down through the years?

Camp Location: 62° 50.27'N 109° 09.36'W
Distance Today: 43 km. paddle, 0 km. portage
Distance to Date: 358 km. paddle, 0 km. portage

The men from Massachusetts fish from their aircraft.

Young inmates of Dog City.

Chapter 5: PIKE'S PURGATORY

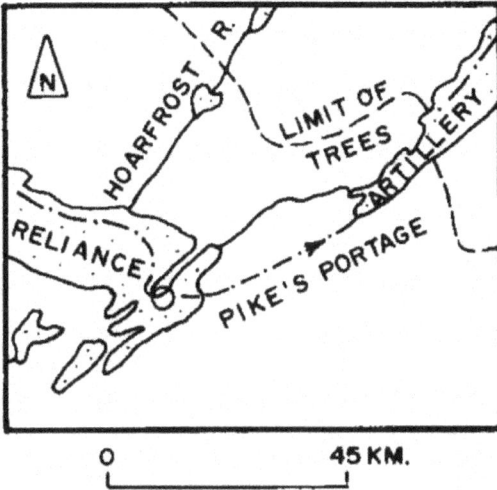

July 12

The southward crossing to Reliance begins on a calm lake, but conditions become choppy as we approach the halfway point, chased by a thunderstorm sweeping in from the west. I'm concerned about our distance from shore, but we pull through without taking on any water. The crossing takes two hours.

As we round Fairchild Point on the far side of the Lake, we meet up with Jerry and Jim, puttering around in an outboard, clad in bright yellow slickers against the rain. They're vacationers, up from Las Vegas to catch fish (a common preoccupation of our American cousins, it seems). On hearing we've paddled the lake from Yellowknife, they invite us to their accommodation at Trophy Lodge in Reliance for a congratulatory cup of coffee. Once on shore, we're joined by Spencer and Richard, who work here. We spend a couple of relaxing hours at the lodge, exchanging tall tales and viewing an extensive collection of photos and clippings describing

Reliance's former role as an outpost of the Royal Canadian Mounted Police. The detachment was closed in 1961. RCMP buildings dating from the 1920s and 30's are still in use by the lodge, including a small hut that used to be a jail.

On July 2nd, 1929, Inspector Charles Trundle, accompanied by Corporal R.A. Williams and Constables Kirk and Bobblets, left this post in two canoes in search of John Hornby. Hornby and two young companions had wintered on the Thelon River, but didn't reappear in the spring. When the Mounties reached the desolate cabin, they discovered the trio's bodies and the diary of Edgar Christian, Hornby's cousin, the last of the three to die of starvation. After scrawling a final farewell to his parents, along with an admonition not to blame Hornby for the tragedy, the clear-thinking teen placed the diary in the cast-iron stove for safekeeping, leaving a note to tell the searchers where to look. Published posthumously under the title "Unflinching," it's a sobering reminder of the occasional cost of adventure.

Spencer and Richard are generous hosts. At their invitation, we use the kitchen in the main lodge to prepare our early meal. It's an attractive, recently constructed log building, pre-assembled in Yellowknife and then shipped out to Reliance by barge. Temporarily reacquainted with the ease of microwave cookery, we enjoy this pleasant change in our routine. While we cook, the conversation continues. Spencer and Richard are both natives of Yellowknife. Spencer attends high school there and can't wait to leave. He says there's nothing to do during the winter. He's spent his summers at Trophy Lodge since the age of four. His current ambition is to become a chef. Richard is in his mid-20s and has also spent a lot of time in the local area. He tells us how to recognize the bottom end of Pike's Portage and describes its condition as "generally good." A local trapper uses it while tending his lines, and Richard has sometimes worked with him.

We ask about a large compound next door to the lodge, containing several orange-painted storage tanks. We're told it used to be part of a meteorological station. The radio masts have been removed, and the whole compound was recently sold by public tender. No one at the lodge knows the identity of the purchaser. Richard says it won't mean competition for Trophy Lodge because a Territorial regulation requires that fishing lodges on Great Slave Lake be separated by many miles of intervening shoreline.

The atmosphere here is friendly, laid-back and quiet, the type of vacation spot I'd enjoy if I didn't have a previous commitment. Apart from the duo from Las Vegas, there are no other paying guests. Richard says most will arrive later in the summer when the fishing's better. Jerry and Jim purposely fly in early, "to get away from the crowds." Unlike the gang we saw back at Plummer's Lodge, their approach to fishing is relaxed rather than fanatical. There are lots of fish in the lake, and they have plenty of time.

Our two-hour lunch break over, it's time to go. Jerry and Jim return to their outboard while Richard walks us to the dock and helps us get underway. We set out through mist and drizzle, and about an hour later, reach the landing at the head of the portage, minds full of the hard work ahead.

Pike's Portage is a formidable undertaking, a 40-kilometre-long chain of eight small lakes with intervening portages leading from the east end of Great Slave Lake, northeast to Artillery Lake. Starting at 513 feet above sea level and ending at an elevation of 1178 feet, it's a gateway to the tundra of the subarctic plateau. Aboriginal people have used it for thousands of years as a passage to the barrens to hunt caribou. In 1834, the Royal Navy's George Back and party used this route while returning from their journey of exploration to the Arctic Ocean at Chantry Inlet. The portage was popularized by Warburton Pike, who wrote about it in the 1890s. Many explorers and adventurers have made use of it since Pike's time. Here's what some of them have had to say about it, starting with Pike himself:

This is by far the prettiest part of the country that I saw in the north, and was looking its best under bright sunshine....

Scattering timber, spruce and birch clothed the sloping banks down to the sandy shores of the lakes; berries of many kinds grew in profusion... A perfect northern fairyland it was... (Pike, 1892)

...we thankfully beached our York boat at the famous lobstick [a tree with the lower branches removed] *that marks the landing of Pike's Portage. Carved on the lobstick were many names famous in the annals of this region, Pike, Mattern, McKinley, Munn, Tyrrell among them. All about were evidences of an ancient and modern camp; lodge poles ready for the covers, relics and wrecks of all sorts, fragments of canoes and sleds, and the inevitable stray...dog.* (Seton, 1907)

Pike's Portage starts with a steep 3½ mile climb to the first lake. I had my instruments and gear and the survey to make. Sousi carried a light pack... Basile carried the canoe. When we reached the first lake, we had to wait some time for Basile. When he arrived, his dark face was such a peculiar muddy colour that I laughed. After some discussion with Basile, Sousi said, "You shouldn't laugh. Basile say he maybe die." (Blanchet, 1924)

Such travellers as go beyond Reliance must take Pike's Portage, a route of alternating ponds, streams, rocks, hills and muskeg. It is a man's route...The second day on the portages was torture. A steady drizzle soaked the muskeg to a mud-like consistency and made the rock slimy. A swarm of black flies completed the misery. (Waldron, 1931)

[The] *last place where Hornby and party were seen alive.* (Whalley, 1980)

Like so many of the places one visits, the character of this portage is malleable, shaped in the mind as well as the eye. One man's northern fairyland is another's misery. A possible reason for Pike's cheery description is that he was moving in the downhill direction, his gear carried by hirelings. He was also on his way home.

Sitting in our canoes at the landing and snapping pictures to delay the inevitable toil, we again find we're not alone. We smell the smoke of a campfire and see movement in the trees, followed by a cheery, "Hello there! Come on in!" It's Hugh, a retired RCMP officer and veteran of many northern postings, Allan, an official with a chemical company, and Susan, Hugh's daughter, a medical doctor. All three are from Western Canada. They were flown to Artillery Lake at the uphill end of the portage and are making a leisurely passage back to Yellowknife. Hugh and Allan paddle a venerable Grumman aluminum canoe, while Susan is using a kayak.

We indulge in a few minutes of light conversation and exchange addresses. The others then wisely retire to their fire to allow us to prepare mentally and physically for the first phase of the portage, a four-and-a-half-kilometre, uphill hike with all one can carry and more, to Harry Lake. Chris has decreed that each crew is responsible for their own boat and gear, so he and I each load up with one canoe, plus a small pack, for a total weight of perhaps 85 pounds apiece. This is the first time I've ever portaged a canoe solo. What a place to learn! It feels as if I'm attempting a grad school exam before finishing kindergarten. Not to be outdone, Jill and Christy struggle into the harnesses of large food packs, weighing in at about 100 pounds each. We mount up and struggle forward on legs rubbery from lack of use. Our friends photograph us as we pass their fire, and promise to send us copies.

From a personal perspective, things don't go well. Moving at our own pace, Jill and I become separated from the others, and although the trail is deeply rutted and generally obvious, the ruts diverge in a few places. Head immersed in jostling Kevlar and sweating profusely under my bug shirt, I manage to take a left fork instead of a right, and I lead Jill astray. About an hour into our ordeal, we realize we've missed the mark. That creek and valley should be on our left, not our right. We set the baggage down and consider our options. At Jill's suggestion, I mark the spot with the GPS. We then leave our burdens, except for my small pack and scout a path back to the start of our unintended detour. When we regain the right path, I decide to carry my small pack ahead to the upper end of the portage, planning to return for the canoe once I have the route figured out. Jill returns to the start of the portage to grab another pack, giving me a chance to find Harry Lake and make things right with the other luggage.

After walking alone for about another hour, I find that the trail diverges again, on a low ridge just west of a buggy marsh. Knowing I'm close to Harry Lake, and unwilling to risk another mistake, I leave my pack on a rusted fuel drum, intending to return to the canoe and Jill's first pack and advance them to my current location. On the way, I meet Chris and Christy, who have by now finished their first crossing uneventfully. Chris tries to persuade me to return with them to the Great Slave end of the trail to enjoy a supper that Hugh and company are cooking for us, using the last of our fresh vegetables. I decline, unable to rest knowing how much work is still ahead.

I find the abandoned canoe and pack, but after my misdirected ramblings over rough terrain, I have little energy to do much else. Ten days of big-lake paddling does wonders for the arms, but is poor training for the art of the portage. I move the canoe and pack forward in relays, using up most of my remaining energy in short bursts of sweaty effort. I make progress, but not much. Conceding this round to the trail, I return to Great Slave Lake for food and conversation, both desperately needed at this point as I am running low on calories and morale. On the way back, I muse that having scattered gear across several square kilometres of wilderness, I now know this small part of the country quite well and could someday serve as a guide here. I imagine myself intoning to some awe-struck tourists, "Not that way! That leads to Dead-End Bog. Why, I recall a time many years ago..."

I reach the Great Slave end of the portage. Later, Jill returns as well, having made her second trip without incident. We join what by now is a lively dinner party. The main course turns out to be an all-you-can-eat helping of thick, rich stew, with extra meat provided by our hosts. There's also tea with real lemon juice, which Allan doles out from a green plastic bottle he keeps in his shirt pocket. I eat and drink slowly but continuously and feel my body respond. Soon, I'm able to enjoy the conversation. Hugh shares stories from his policing in the north. He recalls one case about a husband who told his wife he was visiting an isolated hunting camp, while in reality he was shacking up with his latest female friend. A snowstorm blew in, and his wife got worried and called the Mounties. With great difficulty and expense, the road to the camp was ploughed open at the height of the blizzard. The police found an empty camp, and the man paid the emotional and financial costs of his lie. Hugh also describes his role in assessing the suitability of recruits for isolated, northern service. I recall my father's role in assessing student candidates for the ministry. I wonder if they looked for any of the same qualities.

Later, Jill and I set out for one last go at delivering our initial burdens to the right address. Chris and Christy decide to stay on at the dinner party. I guide Jill to where I left her pack, and then backtrack for the canoe. We resolve to advance our burdens all the way to the top of the portage, but end up setting them down again just short of our destination. I retrieve my small pack from the fuel drum as we pass. We continue, unburdened, to the shore of Harry Lake, where we make our camp using what equipment is available. By the time we finish, it's midnight, and I can barely lift my legs.

So far, this portage has been no northern fairyland. The lakeshore here looks gloomy and dismal in the murky twilight. It's also swampy and bug-infested. Whose idea was this anyway? During the dinner party, Hugh told us he's glad that "young people from the south are coming north to explore and aren't deterred by talk of insects and cold weather." If I had my way, every young person from the south would spend a summer marching up and down Pike's Portage. Whether it would do them any good, I can't say. That's not the point. In my current foul mood, I just want them all to suffer like me. The bright spot is that Jill remains friendly and doesn't hold the mistake against me. Forgiveness is a wonderful gift.

And so, to bed, hoping I don't wake up crippled and that there's breakfast food somewhere in the baggage that has made it this far.

Camp Location: 62° 41.32'N 108°54.58'W
Distance Today: 12 km. paddle, 0 km. portage
Distance to Date: 370 km. paddle, 0 km. portage

July 13

A continuing battle with the first leg of Pike's purgatory. Much pain. Finally, all goods are at Harry Lake. We'll spend a second pleasant evening here, amidst the mud, swarms of bugs, caribou bones and rotted remains of old canoes. Goody! Chris finds a couple of leg-hold traps and demonstrates their use by setting one of them up and triggering it with a stick. The resulting, definitive "clack" sounds like an expletive, a succinct and fitting commentary on this stage of our journey. My Therm-a-Rest mattress is punctured by a sharp stone, and the zipper on my bug shirt fails. Not a good day. Too tired to write.

Camp Location: 62° 41.32'N 108°54.58'W
Distance Today: 0 km. paddle, 4.6 km. portage
Distance to Date: 370 km. paddle, 4.6 km. portage

Editor's Note: All portage distances cited are one-way. Multiply by 3 to obtain the total distance walked. Distances for multi-day portages are recorded on the day the portage was completed.

July 14

We're camped at the south end of Burr Lake, still in the midst of Mr. Pike's "northern fairyland". I'm getting the knack of this portage business and made much better progress today. Chris showed me how to rest the canoe's thwart on top of my small pack, instead of directly on my tortured shoulders. This reduced the pain considerably. Jill performed a miracle cure on my bug shirt. Christy applied a patch to my inflatable mattress, drawn from a repair kit kept in the vast, blue SealLine pack that serves as our utility bag. As John, Paul, George and Ringo once sang, I get by with a little help from my friends.

This evening, we enjoy pan-fried pizza for supper: an excellent blend of bannock dough, sun-dried tomatoes, mozzarella cheese and sliced pepperoni. After the meal, I try to launch a new verbal preoccupation to replace our ongoing and best-left-unmentioned poetry competition. It's hitting too close to home. I have no name for my new word game, but introduce it with the following example: "There's a small spot of gangrene on your elbow," smiled the doctor, **disarmingly**. Our resident literati remain obsessed with their simple, back-end rhymes, and there are few responses. The best of them (according to me) was my own: "The prisoner escaped over the wall using a rope," said the warden, **condescendingly**.

Today's air temperature is 58°F, the coldest yet. Skies are still gloomy with occasional light rain. During our most recent walking and paddling, we've noticed patches of stunted trees as well as open areas that might be considered tundra. In camp, I use our copy of "A Naturalist's Guide to the Arctic" to identify red bearberry and blood-spot lichen.

We hope to make it to Artillery Lake tomorrow and finish this prolonged, intermittent walk.

Camp Location: 62° 47.72'N 108° 36.69'W
Distance Today: 18 km. paddle, 2.2 km. portage
Distance to Date: 388 km. paddle, 6.8 km. portage

Chapter 6: NOCTURNAL ARTILLERY

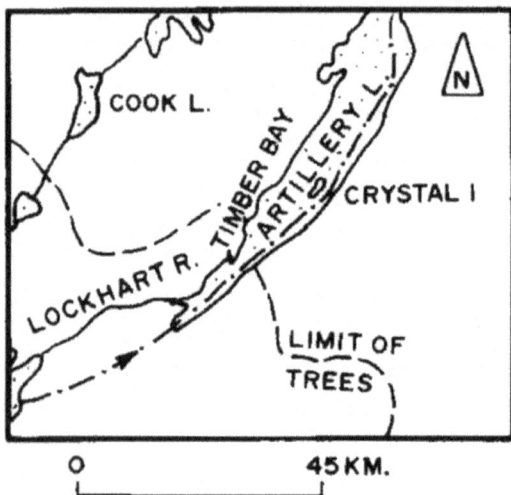

July 15

We completed Pike's Portage today, after more hard work than I ever hope to repeat. Still, the relief at the end of the trail wouldn't have been as sweet without the effort we put into it.

Given its name by George Back "...*out of respect to the distinguished corps* [the Royal Artillery] *to which some of my crew belonged...*" Artillery Lake begins as a narrow, steep-sided bay. With today's breeze from the northeast, it's a funnel of wind. We would probably have been windbound, even had we arrived earlier in the day as planned. Instead, we arrived late in the afternoon, after getting turned around between Burr and Toura Lakes, where we received extra portage practice for our pains: frustrating and disheartening, but no permanent damage to morale. Unfortunately, there's been damage to our equipment. After bouncing on shoulders for the past two days, the thwarts of both canoes have come loose at the place where a vertical aluminum shaft and "foot" connect them to the keel.

Worse, the aluminum cross-piece in Chris and Christy's newer boat broke clean through during today's vigorous exercise.

Chris has applied quick-dry, cold-cure epoxy to Jill's and my canoe and has jury-rigged a thwart for his own, using a small birch log. It's just a temporary fix, and a more permanent solution is needed if that canoe is to make it to the Arctic Ocean. Chris plans to have the necessary parts — aluminum tubing, a hacksaw, and a rivet gun — flown in to a geological camp, a tiny speck of temporary civilization out on the tundra, northeast of Clinton-Colden Lake. By prior arrangement, it's also where we're to pick up our first pre-positioned cache of food.

The bugs (black flies) here at the south end of Artillery Lake are the worst yet. It's too windy for the cook tent, so apart from our bug shirts, we're at their mercy. When we sit down, they swarm around us in excited billows like smoke. Walking around camp, we each carry our own personal pillar of cloud like biblical Israelites wandering the deserts of Sinai. The critters like to spend most of their time in the calm air to the lee of our bodies. Of necessity, we eat facing the wind as masses of agitated insects pelt against our backs like hail. At bedtime, despite our precautions, several hundred follow us into the tents in the few seconds it takes to dive through the flaps and close the zipper. We then spend 20 minutes culling the herd to manageable proportions by patiently smearing tiny bodies against the fabric walls with our fingers, one by one. Realizing their plight, the bugs reconsider their strategy and batter against the taut nylon in a fruitless attempt to escape. We'd gladly let them out if only we could keep more of their friends from coming in. But there's no way to negotiate a withdrawal and no way to accept the surrender of the rapidly thinning remnants of the bugs' expeditionary force. Once the initial urgency is over and the battle won, we hunt down the remainder at our leisure, for sport. We sleep on a thick carpet of dead bugs, but it's better than sleeping with live ones.

The wind drops this evening, and the temperature falls to the point where I put on my toque to keep warm. The barrens will soon be upon us.

Camp Location: 62° 51.25'N 108° 30.62'W
Distance Today: 6 km. paddle, 2.5 km. portage
Distance to Date: 394 km. paddle, 9.3 km. portage

July 16

We break camp and move out at 8:30 a.m., but it's a short-lived effort. Buffeted by a strong headwind, we decide not to fight it, and at 11 a.m., pull over to the western shore. We'll try a nocturnal paddle this evening to recover the lost time. In the meantime, we nap, lounge and read to pass the time. We also build a large bonfire to dispose of an accumulation of our garbage, including an old fly from Chris' tent, which has leaked once too often for its own good. It's disquieting to see how the thin, colourful fabric reacts to flame: it melts, drips and burns like a torch.

By mid-afternoon, the temperature is 60°F in bright sunlight, and the bugs are again swarming, hampered in their malicious intent by the continuing wind.

We're about 3 kilometres south of Timber Bay, so-named because George Back's carpenters found enough wood there to complete the boats he and his crew would use to descend the Great Fish (Back) River to Chantry Inlet. On March 13, 1834, *"...that there might be no leisure for brooding over their privations, I sent Mr. King with the whole of them...to drag the iron work, together with such planking as the carpenters might have ready, to a bay on the western borders of Artillery Lake, where I intended the boats to be built."* Back and his men had endured a long, harsh winter, and he was probably sick of their mutterings and grumblings in their cramped winter quarters on the shore of Great Slave Lake.

Our own leader has different ideas of how to maintain group cohesion. Starting today, Chris has assumed the persona of Christopher Robin and has assigned each of us our own Winnie-the-Pooh names. Christy receives the honour of becoming Pooh, due to her preference for honey at breakfast. Jill becomes Tigger, while I'm stuck with Eeyore. No explanations for these latter choices are offered, and we know better than to ask. I'd rather be the wise old owl, but have no say in the matter. "I'm Christopher Robin, looking after all my little friends!" chirps Chris as he pulls another trout from the lake. It's been said that "who controls the food controls the men." It must be true because I decide that playing a part-time role as a fictional donkey is a fair exchange for regular meals of fresh fish.

Camp Location: 62° 55.28'N 108° 20.00'W
Distance Today: 9 km. paddle, 0 km. portage
Distance to Date: 403 km. paddle, 9.3 km. portage

July 17

Today, we complete a long, nocturnal transit of Artillery Lake, stopping just short of a point near the narrows leading to Ptarmigan Lake. Setting out at 9:30 p.m. on the 16th, we paddle throughout the night, pausing at Beaver Lodge Mountain at about 3 a.m. to refuel. We decide to call this meal breakfast and have pancakes, with butter and corn syrup, washed down with strong, black coffee. We're hungry, but even so, the stomachs of some of us rebel at having food thrown into them at this unusual hour.

I tell Chris that travellers sometimes sprinkled tobacco on the water here, an offering to the great beaver to ensure safe passage. He responds by scattering a handful of his precious, continental blend coffee on the calm, dark water. "For safe passage," he intones, apparently hoping that finely ground beans are as acceptable a currency as dried leaves in the economy of the watching spirits. He then draws out a bundle of sweetgrass, another custom blend. This was assembled for him by Joan, a well-wisher and paddler from his most recent Nahanni River trip. Striking a match, he touches it to the tightly bound tuft of vegetation and holds it aloft to salute the lake once more. Conversation stops as we watch the aromatic smoke curl gently upward. It's a special moment. The profound silence, the dimly lit vault of open sky, the reddish-gold band rimming the distant horizon and the incense hovering like mist in the cool air comprise a setting as sacred as any cathedral. I bypass the beaver, the lake spirits and all the other middlemen and pray directly to God in Heaven, because I know he hears me when I do.

During the extended twilight joining the 16th and the 17th of July, we leave the land of trees behind and enter the realm of the barrens. It's not an abrupt transition, more of a band than a line. We encountered occasional patches of tundra as far back as the middle of Pike's Portage and will no doubt continue to see a few stunted trees. Based on our prior research, we know that in this part of the subarctic, the zone of transition is not parallel to a line of latitude; instead, it follows a northwest-southeast trend. Our "Naturalist's Guide" cites the influence of Hudson Bay as the reason. The bay freezes over in the winter and thaws in the summer, absorbing much of the summer's heat in the process. This depresses summer temperatures over a wide swath of the adjacent country. Trees can grow in the cooler climate, but their seeds won't germinate. The "tree line" is a result. On a less informative vein, I recall a recent story in the Globe and Mail newspaper about an anticipated northward shift of the tree line caused by climate change. In describing this effect, the author, with apparently only a loose grasp of the concept, made a startling claim: *"When a tree becomes sexually active, it can move at the rate of 100 metres per year."* We've yet to notice any post-pubescent vegetation shuffling slowly northward in search of a pollination partner.

The calm holds, so we continue our efforts well into the next day, completing a respectable 74-kilometre, 24-hour run, including a pause for a nap 10 kilometres north of Crystal Island.

During the daylight hours of the 17th, Chris and Christy realize that they've left our dip net at a rest stop about five kilometres back, near Twin Buttes Point. Since fish are impossible to haul into the canoe without it, they have little choice but to turn back. Jill and I continue northward, on the understanding that we'll only go as far as the outlet of the Lockhart River, at the lake's north end.

Without the other canoe to goad and motivate us, our pace slows considerably. It's a relief to relax and dabble along at a snail's pace. In canoeing parlance, this is known as "lily dipping," and coming on the heels of our recent hard work, I like it a lot. The sky is deep blue, the air is warm and calm, and the water is transparent and tranquil, tinted with reflected light. Taking an inside passage between the lake's eastern shore and a small island, we skim across a shallow, sandy bay. The lake's transparency makes it seem as if we're paddling in air, gliding smoothly above the golden sand that churns and sparkles in our wake. Ripple marks on the sandy bottom are intricate and greatly pleasing to the eye. On a deeper part of the lake, I look down through clear, cold, magnifying layers of water to see three large trout, hovering about 10 to 15 feet below. They scatter, startled as the wedge-shaped shadow of our silent craft skims across the rocky bottom like a manta ray.

A couple of hours later, our thirst for independence satisfied, Jill and I pull over to wait for the others. I place my bright orange toque on the end of my paddle and wedge it upright between some rocks on top of a low hill, as a marker and guide. When the others finally rejoin us, I wait to be complimented for my thoughtfulness, but no mention is made of my signal. When I finally ask when they first saw the marker, it turns out that they hadn't noticed it at all and had only seen Jill and me when we were just a few hundred metres away. I take this lesson to heart. It's a big country up here. I don't ever plan to stray too far from camp.

The notes scrawled on the margins of my map testify that many explorers and adventurers have visited this part of the subarctic over the years. I enjoy reading about their experiences and impressions as we briefly inhabit the same space. Just a few kilometres northwest of tonight's camp, two

English adventurers, John Hornby and James Critchell-Bullock, "...spent a winter of unnecessary discomfort and danger in a cave dug in the side of an esker" in the mid-1920s. They had quarrelled with their companions, who took the tents when they parted. In the middle of that long, cold winter, Hornby made a trip down to the RCMP post at Reliance for supplies and hinted to the constable there that his roommate was trying to kill him. This was apparently meant as a joke, but it did not amuse Critchell-Bullock or the Mounties, who subsequently paid them a visit. In the end, no one killed anyone, although as already noted, Hornby starved to death a few years later, on the Thelon River. Skipping farther back along the timeline, I find that we're at roughly the same location as George Back and company as they made their way up the Lockhart River on June 15th, 1834: *"We encamped under the shelter of a rocky hill about a quarter mile from the river...Divine service having been read to the men assembled in the tent, the journey was resumed by line of the river."* The next day, Back's party had a little excitement on the same part of the Lockhart we hope to traverse tomorrow:

On arriving at the first rapid, some trouble and waste of time were experienced in ascending its contracted and furious torrent. Once the boat grounded, the line broke and only by jumping out was the bowman enabled to save her from being driven on the rocks; and such was the immense force of the water that it was not until she was lightened of her cargo that the men succeeded in hauling her up...Carron broke through [the ice] and sunk over his head: his next companion... instantly seized him by the arm and saved him from being swept away by the current.

May our own passage be less dramatic.

Camp Location: 63° 24.58'N 107° 37.10'W
Distance Today: 74 km. paddle, 0 km. portage
Distance to Date: 477 km. paddle, 9.3 km. portage

Somewhere in the middle of Pike's Portage.

The east end of Pike's Portage at Artillery Lake.

Midnight silence on Artillery Lake.

A lonely canoe on Ptarmigan Lake.

Chapter 7: SOME DEEP PHILOSOPHICAL QUESTIONS

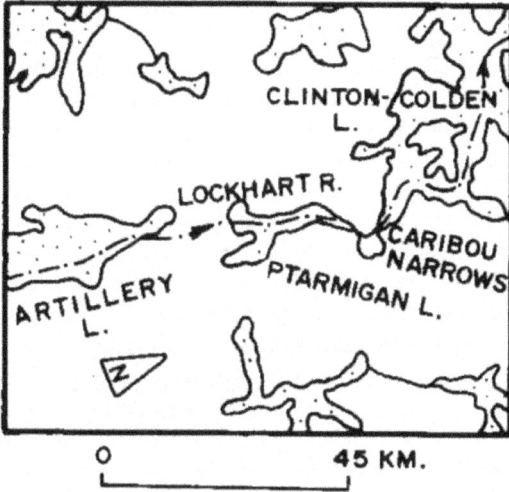

July 18

Our Lockhart River experience is indeed less dramatic than Back's. We don't have spring runoff or ice to contend with and are able to paddle against the current with little difficulty. We complete three brief portages at rapids, the longest about 500 metres, and then continue up Ptarmigan Lake to Caribou Narrows, where we stop for the night.

Ptarmigan Lake gives us a tentative connection with Samuel Hearne. Between 1770 and 1772, he travelled overland from Fort Prince of Wales (modern-day Churchill) to the Coppermine River and back again. He actually made three journeys; the first ended in 1769 when his guides deserted him, the second in 1770, when his quadrant (survey instrument) blew over and was broken. The third, successful attempt began later that same year. Hearne's exact route remains a matter of debate, but it seems we're close to it today. According to an annotated version of his journal prepared by the Champlain

The Hummingbird from Resolute

Society in 1911...

...the map shows that their course was across Partridge Lake...It is a small lake on the river between Artillery and Clinton-Colden Lakes, and lies just a little north of the southern edge of the barren lands. The name given to it on the Cook map is Cossadgath and on the Mackenzie map Cassandgath Lake, which are evidently modifications of the Chipewyan word for Ptarmigan or White Partridge.

We're now well within the barrens, that immense arctic prairie where tundra vegetation predominates. There can be no adequate mental preparation for the dissolution of our familiar frame of reference. Without trees, distances are hard to judge. Headlands only a few canoe lengths away appear distant and remote, while clusters of rolling, rock-studded hills, apparently close at hand, still linger in front of us an hour's hard paddle after we first lay eyes on them. We expected dazzling carpets of arctic flowers, but few are in evidence. The primary terrestrial colours are muted browns, greens and greys. Lichens coat the angular rocks on the high, dry ridges, while mosses and heaths are found lower down. Dense thickets of dwarf birches and willows line the lake shores. They also form linear patches along creeks and gullies that occupy cracks and faults in the bedrock. Intermittent stands of stunted, knee-high white spruce occupy sheltered patches of sandy soil. In the absence of wind and our own conversation, the silence is almost overwhelming.

Always looking for ways to encourage and entertain his companions, Chris has taken to crooning something he calls "a cowboy song." It starts out promisingly enough: "All through the day, in the saddle I sway..." and I have heard worse voices. Unfortunately, that single line is all he knows of the tune, and the crooning soon becomes...redundant. The rest of us are loath to discourage a budding musical talent, so we don't voice this concern, silently hoping that the rest of the tune, or at least another line, will eventually emerge.

Two interesting biological facts I learned from my fellow travellers today: 1) seagulls can't burp, so if you feed them enough Alka-Seltzer, they'll explode; and 2) rat poison works only because rats can't vomit. A lifetime of learning continues.

Camp Location: 63° 40.90'N 107° 19.91'W
Distance Today: 32 km. paddle, 1.5 km. portage
Distance to Date: 509 km. paddle, 10.8 km. portage

July 19

This evening we're camped on the north side of Clinton-Colden Lake after a 49-kilometre run, good paddling considering that we didn't start until about 10 a.m.

Early in our paddling day, as we enter Clinton-Colden Lake, we pass a landmark on the east side of Caribou Narrows that had special significance for Seton during his 1907 expedition:

On the afternoon of August 9 we passed an important headland that I have called Tyrell Point. Here we jumped off his map into the unknown. I had of course the small chart drawn by Sir George Back in 1834 but it was hastily made under great difficulties and with few exceptions it seemed impossible to recognize his landscape features.

On September 5th, 1855, Anderson and Stewart were headed in the opposite direction after an unsuccessful search for the remnants of Franklin's fatal 1845 expedition. They, too, were wrestling with Back's map as they sought to find this same Caribou Narrows. Anderson vented his frustration in his journal: *"The whole day has been spent in looking for the river. Back's small map is a snare and a delusion...I trust never to be guided by such a map... again."*

The navigational skills required for our present journey differ from those needed by earlier explorers. While we study maps produced from satellite images and aerial photography, they studied the land and water, sometimes with the help of Aboriginal guides or crude sketch maps. While the old charts often disappointed those attempting to rely on them, we can be reasonably sure our modern maps are accurate. Our task is to judge distances while matching the contours and shorelines on the map with the features we see around us. Chris has proven to be highly proficient in this. I often refer to my own set of maps to make sure I have at least a general idea of our location, but I share my opinion only when asked; navigational decisions should never be founded on the resolutions of debating societies. If necessary, we can deploy our secret weapon, a Garmin GPS kept in a small, blue waterproof case secured behind my seat. So far, we've only used it to record our camp locations and measure our cruising speed.

Despite our modern maps and satellite navigation, we're still able to profit from the knowledge of those who went before. Partway up Clinton-Colden Lake, we read what Warburton Pike wrote more than 100 years ago: *"For the benefit of future travellers, I may state that there is a peculiar conical butte...it is just visible above the horizon and is a capital leading landmark..."* We equate this with a feature labelled on our maps as Back's Butte, and this helps us refine our northward course.

Another feature shown on my map is less helpful: a bit of grey shading along part of the lake shore with the annotation "NB." I had cut off part of the legend while trimming the sheet to fit the map case, so there's no help to be had there. After some deliberation, Chris suggests that it signifies a nude beach. We scan the adjacent shoreline expectantly, but find no evidence to support this hypothesis. This doesn't necessarily disprove Chris's theory. There's a time-honoured question about sounds made by falling trees in uninhabited forests. To this I now add: Is a nude beach still a nude beach when no nude people are lounging on it? Hmm...

While passing east of the lake's large, central island, we sight two small clusters of about a half dozen musk oxen, separated from each other by the narrow strait between the island and the mainland. They're quite vocal, each group snorting, stomping and bellowing across the water at the other. We attempt to join in the conversation, snorting and bellowing back at them, but to no noticeable effect. Their belligerence can probably be attributed to the mid-summer rutting season when, according to our Naturalist's Guide, *"a bull, with a harem of cows, will have to defend his supremacy many times against intruding bulls"* and occasional, invading tourists.

The hot sun of the past few days has given way to clouds and gusts of wind this evening. There's a good chance of rain tonight. Chris caught four trout while trolling, and we had them for supper.

Camp Location: 64° 01.70'N 107° 21.25'W
Distance Today: 49 km. paddle, 0 km. portage
Distance to Date: 558 km. paddle, 10.8 km. portage

Chapter 8: ENJOYING VODKA

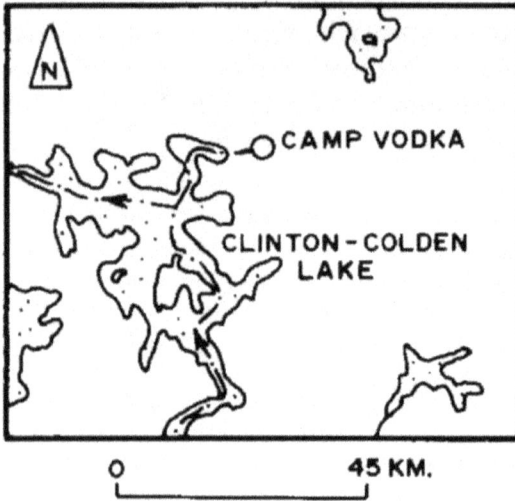

July 20

Editor's Note: On this date, the expedition reached Gerle Gold's Vodka Lake Exploration Camp. Evidently, the author was too distracted to complete a journal entry. Distances travelled are recorded below:

Camp Location: 64° 06.50'N 107° 12.00'W
Distance Today: 19 km. paddle, 1.5 km. portage
Distance to Date: 577 km. paddle, 12.3 km. portage

July 21

We arrived at Gerle Gold's "Camp Vodka" yesterday afternoon, after a confusing passage through a maze of islands and channels in the northeast corner of Clinton-Colden Lake and a difficult hike over fields of scattered boulders. We travelled lighter than usual, leaving the canoes and most of our luggage at the lakeshore before walking the final one and a half kilometres to the camp.

This tiny settlement and adjacent "Lake Vodka" are informally named in honour of Vladimir and Yuri, the two Russian geologists who make up 40% of the camp's population. Despite the company's name, they're looking for diamonds. We're here for treasure of a different sort: a cache of food already waiting for us, plus canoe repair materials to be flown in via a regular supply flight. Yesterday, Chris managed to contact Gerle Gold's Yellowknife office via the camp's shortwave radio. Their busy staff agreed to track down the necessary parts and will put them on today's flight, due to arrive this evening. That's quick service. I think it helped that the office manager in Yellowknife is a rabid canoe enthusiast who understands our requirements. In the meantime, we have the day off to reorganize our expanded food supply. We also have an opportunity to mail a few postcards and possibly use the satellite telephone, which is currently not functioning due to unknown technical issues.

Looking around, it's easy to see that Camp Vodka is a multicultural community. A signboard in front of the kitchen tent, decorated with two empty vodka bottles, proudly proclaims "Kamp Bodka" in Cyrillic lettering. There are bilingual notices (Russian and English) posted at key locations, including one attached to the outhouse door explaining the importance of keeping it firmly closed.

The imported Russians are applying their special skills to the hunt for gems in the Canadian north. They collect soil samples and pan them to reveal concentrations of heavy, indicator minerals. This information can then be mapped and used to trace the locations of old volcanic pipes, where diamonds can sometimes be found. Vladimir says most of these pipes tend to be found under lake water, since they erode more easily than the surrounding rocks.

Natives of Arkhangelsk, Yuri and Vladimir's English isn't perfect, but we're able to communicate with little difficulty. Vladimir is what most people would consider an archetypal Russian: tall, broad-shouldered, bearded, dark brown hair tinged with silver, a deep voice and piercing blue eyes. He's the more outgoing of the two (or his English is better). Yuri is smaller and fairer with a higher-pitched voice. He responds to every question we put to him with the prefix, "of course."

"Do you like hockey, Yuri?"

"Of course, I watch hockey games."

"Do you have children, Yuri?"

"Of course, I have two children."

Mark, the camp cook, and Shannon, the manager, are friendly and hospitable, and after our initial shyness, we're beginning to relax. Due to Chris's earlier arrangements, they were expecting us, but thought we would be a party of eight. I think they're relieved. They fed us a spaghetti dinner last night and bacon with eggs this morning. In return for this generosity, we've tried to make ourselves useful by washing dishes, moving soil samples to the lake for panning, burning garbage, and emptying the ashes from the burn barrel. Those of us with special talents are employed in the kitchen; Jill and Christy are creating a raspberry trifle for the camp's dessert tonight. Apart from these few tasks, it's been a lazy day so far.

The satellite phone comes online in the afternoon. I call my parents' home, but get no answer. I then call friends Jeff and Heather in Markham and speak with them for about 10 minutes, asking them to forward a message to my parents that all is well. I then write a few postcards: "Having a fine time...arms are getting longer, ha ha...send bug repellent," etc. The others are also busy phoning and scribbling.

Later, a phone call from Yellowknife relays the news that the chartered Air Tindi floatplane isn't available. Instead, the helicopter based here at Camp Vodka will fly a round trip to Yellowknife this evening. Once we receive our special delivery, Chris will try to repair the thwart of his canoe in time for a slightly delayed departure tomorrow morning. With time on our hands, we've carefully gone through our personal gear and weeded out things we either haven't used or no longer need. They'll be flown back to Yellowknife and held there until we return. We'll be thankful come the next portage. Regularly forced to carry all our belongings on our backs, we know that every ounce counts.

It's a sunny day, warm and windy, with few insects to bother us. It's peaceful here. A gentle swishing of blades from a small, pole-mounted wind turbine is the loudest sound, accompanied by the occasional, muted rumble and toot from the camp's temporary plumbing. This outpost is an elaborate setup, which I hope to describe in more detail before I finish this entry.

Late in the afternoon, the camp's helicopter leaves to pick up Yuri, Vladimir and Shannon from their remote work location. When they return, Mark will serve us the large turkey he's been cooking all afternoon. Already, the sumptuous aroma of roast bird is everywhere, making it difficult for me to concentrate on my journal. I'm sitting on the ground in front of the kitchen tent, so as not to miss any of the action, culinary or otherwise.

Now to the promised description of Camp Vodka's physical assets. I'll start with the power supply. Electricity is obtained from three separate but linked sources: solar panels, a diesel generator, and that small, busily spinning wind turbine. These feed into a bank of 12-volt batteries that power the lights, computers, and a water heater (yesterday, we enjoyed our first hot shower in about three weeks). There's also a propane oven, refrigerator, coffee percolator, and most of the other comforts of home.

It's 5:04 p.m. and the helicopter has returned. Almost dinnertime! I'll write faster.   The toilet is a vault privy (outhouse). There's a windsock on top so patrons with good bowel control can hold off until the wind is favourable. Kevin, the helicopter pilot, may also find it helpful in planning take-offs and landings. Used toilet paper is deposited in a metal drum and burned to prolong the life of the hole...But that's probably more than you wanted to know. Other structures include a kitchen tent/dining hall, a utility tent (showers, electrical system, water reservoir and general storage), an office tent (phone, desks, computers), and two bunkhouse tents. Shannon has her own small dome tent pitched a few hundred metres away, a personal suburban refuge for those times when she needs to escape the bustle of the central business district. When not ferrying geologists, the camp's helicopter rests on an informal helipad, a high, level patch of ground just north of downtown. There's the inevitable cache of several 45-gallon drums of aviation fuel and a wooden dock at the lake for receiving floatplanes.

No civilization would be complete without indoor plumbing, and this isolated Vodkopolis is no exception. A gasoline-powered pump sucks water from the lake to a holding tank in the utility tent, which serves the showers, water heater and kitchen tent through a network of plastic pipes. As mentioned, this system sometimes makes interesting noises when too many demands are placed on it at once. The occasional ringing of the satellite telephone now adds to the aura of civilization. But it's all temporary. No trace will be left behind once the summer exploration season ends in September. The decommissioning will be done by G&G Expediting of Yellowknife, who flew everything in and assembled it, for a price. (Come on, guys, let's eat!)

It's strange, but even after all the work it took to get here, the four of us will be happy to leave this comfortable oasis and head out on our own again. Our summer's purpose is to travel, and sitting idle makes us uneasy. Chris, in particular, is anxious to leave, a fact he relates to me on several occasions. He's appeased somewhat by Mark's tin of tobacco and stock of cigarette paper. Chris's resolve to give up his occasional habit has crumbled, and now he bums a smoke whenever Mark enjoys one. Chris is gradually learning the ins and outs of rolling a well-stuffed cigarette. How will he behave once separated from his supplier of nicotine? I suppose we'll...Dinner time! Gotta go!

It's now after dinner. The chopper has left on the first leg of its round trip to Yellowknife. The conversation was good, the food was great, and I'm too sleepy to write any more.

Camp Location: 64° 06.50'N 107° 12.00'W
Distance Today: 0 km. paddle, 0 km. portage
Distance to Date: 577 km. paddle, 12.3 km. portage

July 22

More waiting today. The helicopter didn't return from Yellowknife last night, so we sit around camp with our gear packed up and ready to go. Shannon, Yuri and Vladimir are down by the lake, panning the accumulated soil samples that Chris and I moved there yesterday. Their means of transport isn't available, so this is their only geological task for the day. They work through lunch and knock off early.

The anticipated return of the wayward helicopter is repeatedly updated from "mid-morning," to "noon," to "mid-afternoon," to "after supper." We fill the day by reading and rereading old copies of the Globe and Mail and Edmonton Sun, along with some of the books we brought with us. I retrieve a thick Wilbur Smith novel from the pile to be sent back and dive into it. It's about slave traders and adventurers in Africa, one of those stories with a large cast of characters that spans several generations. Given our current setting, I can't get into it. We continue to wash dishes and help out with camp chores whenever we can. There's no evidence that our continued presence is annoying our hosts, but we need to get moving. We've got such a long way to go. For now, it's clear we're staying for at least another night, so we unpack our things and pitch our tents again, this time beside the kitchen tent instead of further out on the tundra as before.

After the evening meal, Shannon encourages Vladimir to tell us his "mosquito joke." He grins mischievously and proceeds in a deep-voiced, heavily accented English: "A geologist is in his tent. He tries to be sleeping, but there is one tiny mosquito inside with him." Here Vladimir pauses and gives a good imitation of the whining hum of a bug on the prowl. He continues, "The geologist gets up from bed. He puts out his hand and speaks to the mosquito: 'Come, little mosquito...you are tired? Come, little one. Come and rest here in my hand.' The mosquito comes and rests on the geologist's hand. The geologist tenderly rocks the mosquito until it sleeps." Vladimir then leans forward towards the imaginary mosquito sleeping in his outstretched palm and whines irritatingly into its tiny, imaginary ear. He smiles modestly at the resultant laughter. Apparently, both Russians are heavily into humour, particularly of the political kind, which, as Vladimir explains, was suppressed until the coming of perestroika and glasnost. Shannon confirms that laughter is often heard emanating from the Russians' tent late into the night, as they devour political joke books imported from their homeland.

After a final glass of Mott's Clamato juice, to which they both appear addicted, the two Russians retire early to their bunkhouse and their joke books. Mark slides "The Ultimate Best of Johnny Cash" into the CD player, and we're transported back to the sixties on the notes spun out by the man in black. Topics of conversation include Shannon's houseboat in Yellowknife harbour (it's painted purple and has an old snowplough blade for an anchor), first movies seen in theatres, old TV shows, childhood memories, environmental issues in northern mining, and so on. Mark shows us his collection of musk oxen hair, gathered from the tundra outside camp. He says it's prized for its insulating properties and sells for around $100 a pound. The Inuit call it qiviut. Now that we know how to recognize it, maybe we'll start our own collection.

The chopper finally shows up around 10:15 p.m. It's piloted by Kevin, who was happy to visit his wife and baby in Yellowknife, but is tired after his long day and goes directly to bed. Chris gathers our repair materials. He and I pound flat the ends of a hollow, rectangular bar of aluminum, turning it into a replacement thwart. Chris decides we should make a spare in case another thwart breaks, a reasonable precaution given the many portages still ahead.

Camp Location: 64° 06.50'N 107° 12.00'W
Distance Today: 0 km. paddle, 0 km. portage
Distance to Date: 577 km. paddle, 12.3 km. portage

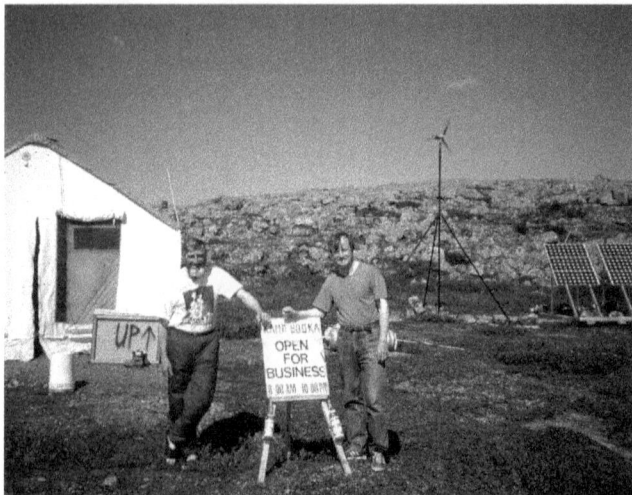

Vladimir and Yuri welcome us to Camp Vodka.

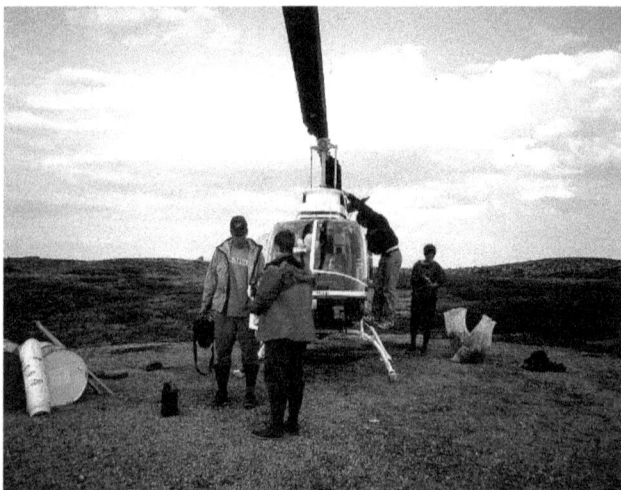

Preparing to leave Camp Vodka the easy way.

Chapter 9: DOUGHNUTS, BEANS AND URIC ACID

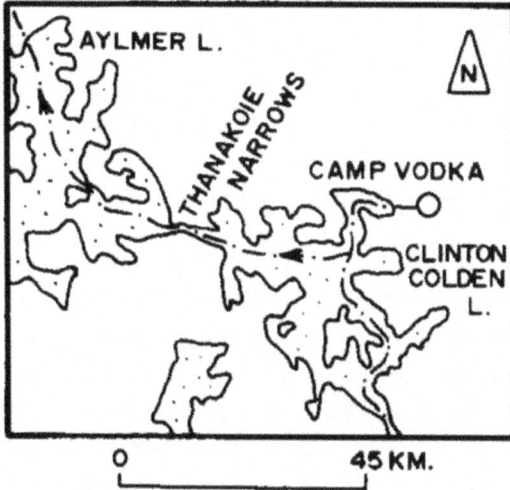

July 23

Away today, finally. Treated royally to the last, we're ferried the short distance back to our canoes by helicopter. It's a first for Jill, Christy and me, so Kevin briefs us on how to enter and leave the machine: "Keep low because the main rotor can tilt suddenly. Keep away from the tail rotor. Exit towards the front so I can keep you in visual contact." He's thorough and professional. Kevin carries Christy and Chris over first and then returns for Jill and me. Over the engine noise in the cockpit, he yells, "This is the best way to travel the barrens!" For the hurried rich, he's probably right. Our knee-straining, boulder-hopping hike of a few days ago becomes a two-minute, armchair adventure. From the air, we marvel at the extent of the boulder fields that dominate the area like the ruins of an immense city, pulverized by jackhammers. When the Apocalypse comes, I doubt the scenery here will change much.

After dropping us off and taxiing Shannon and the

Russians out to their work station, Kevin flies back to the canoes, this time with extra tools and equipment for our use. Once it's apparent that our refit is under control, he climbs back into his machine. The main rotor bites deeply into the cool morning air, and he's off with a thumping roar. The noise fades, and our ears ring as the unmitigated silence of the tundra returns.

Installing the replacement thwart takes most of the morning. When the repairs are complete, we leave the borrowed tools on a high rock in a white plastic bucket for Kevin to pick up later.

We enter the canoes at about 11 a.m. and pull our way towards the main body of Clinton-Colden Lake, full of renewed energy and purpose. An hour later, we're huddled on an island, windbound, experiencing the heaviest rainfall I can recall. Fortunately, we landed, got the tents up, and everything battened down before it hit. After the squall passes, we notice a sharp demarcation between the sunny sky to the south and the dark, low-lying clouds that envelop us. As of 1:20 p.m., the rain has ended, but strong gusts continue, so we sit in our respective tents, contemplating the last few days and speculating about the next few weeks, especially the intensive round of portaging that will begin once we reach the north end of Aylmer Lake.

At 6:45 p.m., we try cooking our supper outdoors; it's too windy to set up the high-peaked cook tent. But the heavy rain returns, and we're soon driven back into the bedroom tents. The sky is sullen, and the temperature is dropping.

Two hours later, it's still raining and windy. By now our stomachs are rumbling, so Chris and Christy decide to cook supper in the vented vestibule of Chris's tent. I'm bedecked in Gore-Tex, awaiting the call to fetch Jill's and my share, so we can eat it in our own less spacious abode: less spacious, but still dry. Such weather is a real test of equipment, and so far, this little house on the tundra is meeting the challenge. I'll check the guy lines and pegs when I venture out. In the meantime, I'll pen some random reflections to help keep my mind off my appetite. It's a strategy that worked well when waiting for that turkey dinner a few days ago.

Keen observers of bug behaviour (know your enemy), we've noticed that those getting into the tents, usually more than a few, tend to gather on the parts of the fabric walls closest to the blue segments of the blue and yellow tent fly. We've concluded it's because the darker segments absorb more solar heat, so the bugs park there to enjoy the warmth. It's been said that understanding leads to respect, and respect is the beginning of affection. Not so with blood-sucking insects. As recorded earlier, we kill them all. Like Colonel Kurtz in "Apocalypse Now," we've learned to kill without passion and without judgment. The blood of thousands is on our hands and smeared in countless dots and lines throughout the interior of the tent. Where we've been tardy, brief streaks of our own blood, squeezed from the bodies of our tiny, winged victims, add to the slaughterhouse décor. Tonight's island home is bug-free, thanks to the wind and rain, so for now, there's no killing to be done. But we're always ready.

On the tundra, bugs are bad, but boots are good. One of our most valuable pieces of equipment so far has been our high-top "Bean Boots," also known as Maine hunting shoes, ordered from the venerable L.L. Bean Company of Freeport. They have a gum rubber sole and bottom, triple stitched to a supple leather upper, extending to just below the knee. They're equipped with long, leather laces, threaded through 14 pairs of brass eyelets. This footwear was on Chris's list of mandatory equipment, and by now it's easy to see why. The thin resin coating on our Kevlar canoes won't stand up to repeated grindings over the rocky landings of these northern lakes and rivers, so we do a fair bit of wading while loading and unloading. When well-greased with periodic applications of a commercial preparation of beeswax and oil, and worn over thick woollen socks, our tall leather boots keep our feet snug and dry. The tight, high lacing protects us even when the water level approaches our knees. With water temperatures sometimes in the low 40s, this is no small consideration. The leather uppers will leak if subjected to prolonged immersion, but they work well enough when we hop in and out, and are far more comfortable than rubber boots. They also offer the necessary ankle support and traction for bog-slogging and rock-hopping with heavy loads. To maximize our comfort, we switch to light hiking shoes when in camp. This gives our well-used Beans a chance to dry out. Some of the people we encountered over the past few weeks commented on the businesslike or even military appearance of our "jackboots," but no one questioned their utility. Hugh, Allan and Susan even complained that using them in the swamp and muskeg of Pike's Portage was cheating. So be it. Who says adventure has to be fair?

Another essential is our set of four large, insulated Tim Horton "Super Tim" coffee mugs, crafted in some far-off Asian land from the finest white plastic, for the Aladdin Corporation. Their bright red handles and red snap-on lids enhance both their visibility and utility. They each hold half a litre of whatever liquid is on hand and can be knocked over without spilling the lot. After I was forced by dire emergency to urinate in one of them during an extended paddling session on choppy water, Jill has been careful to keep track of "which is which," settling on a mug distinctively deformed by the heat of a long-forgotten campfire, as her own. I try not to make a habit of tinkling in my drinking mug, but better that than explode in a sodden whoosh. I now know that my bladder capacity is just less than half a litre. I've filed this bit of physiological trivia in the recesses of my brain along with my shoe size and social insurance number.

Dinner's finally ready at 10 p.m.: some kind of thick, tubular pasta, which no doubt has a proper name, garnished with melted cheese, pepperoni slices and sun-dried tomatoes. We devour it. I wash up during a lull in the rain.

Camp Location: 64° 06.10'N 107° 17.52'W
Distance Today: 5 km. paddle, 0 km. portage
Distance to Date: 582 km. paddle, 12.3 km. portage

July 24

The rain has gone and the winds have diminished, so we take a chance on an 8:30 a.m. departure. This proves to be a good decision because it's dead calm by the time we regain the main body of Clinton-Colden. Mid-morning, a twin-engine Beechcraft appears overhead and begins droning back and forth above the lake in a purposeful pattern like a mechanical vulture waiting for something to die. Chris thinks it must be Charles, a pilot involved in an airborne magnetometer survey. He and Chris met in a Yellowknife doughnut shop the day before we set out. It's a big country up here, but evidently a small society. Chris opens his grey waterproof case, switches on the VHF radio and tunes it to 126.7 MHz, the general aviation frequency.

"Is that you, Charles?" he asks abruptly, without any preamble or explanation.

After a brief pause, "Affirmative" crackles from the radio, presumably from the aircraft we see above us.

"It's Chris. Did you bring us any doughnuts?"

There's a much longer pause, and then "Negative" emerges from the speaker. There's no further contact. Disappointed by this succinct dismissal, Chris reluctantly switches off and packs his radio away. Doughnuts will not rain down on us from a clear, blue sky. Too bad. That would have merited a "Worship me" pose, for sure.

There's another food-related disappointment. I've lost my long-anticipated free meal in Yellowknife. Sitting in the canoe after breakfast and adjusting my position before taking up my life jacket, I don't notice Chris reaching stealthily for his 35mm camera. I spot him only as he raises it to aim and fire. I grope frantically for the jacket, but my sharp reflexes are no match for his autofocus and three-frames-per-second power winder. My meal is gone. To add insult to injury, Jill and Christy each snatch up their own cameras and fire away, claiming that Chris hadn't specified that only the first photo is worth $10. To stop the madness, I promptly slap a $10 royalty on any and all photos of me, regardless of position or clothing. The last I heard, the whole thing had been sent to arbitration.

The combination of cool temperatures and calm water makes for good paddling, and we soon reach Thanakoie Narrows. We take a break at the foot of a small, conical hill on an island in the central part of the strait. This will allow Chris to fillet his most recent catch. He now seems able to land fish at will. The rest of us cheer him on, happily addicted to the taste of fresh trout, fried in butter and sprinkled with lemon pepper or cayenne seasoning.

There's history here. I climb the small hill to stretch my legs and stand where Back and his companions stood on August 26th, 1833:

From its summit we were surprised to behold another immense lake...This splendid sheet of water received the appellation of Lake Aylmer, in honour of the Governor-General of Canada to whose kindness and consideration I felt myself particularly indebted.

Seton made a camp here on August 28th, 1907, and tried a practical joke on his companions:

As Billy and Weso were in their tents having an afternoon nap, I thought it would be a good joke to stampede the caribou on top of them, so I waited behind a rock, intending to jump out as soon as the caribou were past me...I leapt out with horrid yells, but instead of dashing to the tents, they plunged into the deep water, then calmly swam for the other shore.

There are no caribou to stampede today, just scattered old bones, remnants of past, successful hunts.

We stop for the night on an island seven kilometres west of the narrows. After stuffing ourselves with fresh trout and watching the sunset, we crash in our tents at 11 p.m.

Camp Location: 64° 06.06'N 108° 13.13'W
Distance Today: 58 km. paddle, 0 km. portage
Distance to Date: 640 km. paddle, 12.3 km. portage

Chapter 10: PAIN CAN ONLY HURT YOU IF YOU LET IT

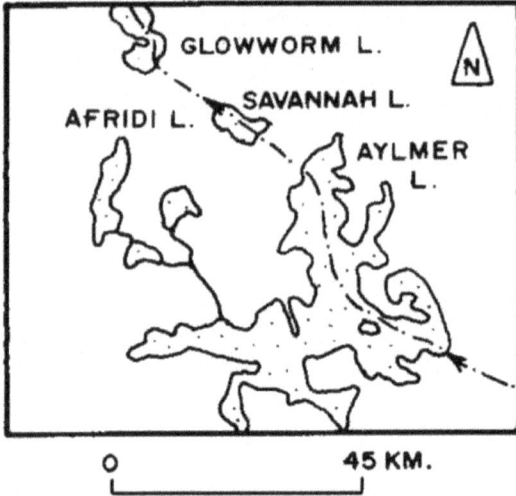

July 25

Good paddling weather again today, and we take full advantage, finishing our passage of Aylmer Lake and starting up a small, unnamed river towards Savannah Lake. As is so often the case with these small, northern streams, the optimistic blue line on the map greatly overstates the paddling potential of the disjointed collection of damp rocks and scattered pools we must navigate. We do a lot of bumping and grinding through shallows, sometimes walking alongside the boats or lifting them over slippery boulders. The volume of water is so small that it's difficult to work out the direction of flow.

When not paddling or dragging loaded canoes over rocks, we're hauling our gear on our shoulders. As I squat on the ground and wriggle my shoulders into the straps of a large, rubber dry bag (I can never find the second strap once my arm is safely through the first), I'm reminded of John Hornby's colourful take on the art of the tundra portage:

Packing is a matter of guts. It is also a matter of back and shoulders and legs. It is a process peculiar to the far places. Civilization has no counterpart for it. The bulky chap who helps juggle pianos in a city would likely find his legs turning to custard and his back giving up, the first hour on the trail. Muskeg has a devilish habit of sucking down one foot and throwing a man off balance. Ropes and straps grow to feel like newly sharpened bandsaws on the longer treks. Even the ability to stagger along with a hundred and a half pounds is only the half of it. Getting the pack on your back comes first...you lie on your side with your back against the pack. The pack may be the size and shape of a 5 foot baked potato, or it may be compact. At any rate, it has straps or ropes tied around it. You grasp those ropes and bring them over your shoulder or over both shoulders if there are two ropes. Then you curl your legs up as far as they'll go and with the aid of your arms, your back, your stomach and most of the rest of the muscles of your body, roll over on your knees. After that it is merely a matter of getting to your feet.

Using these words as inspiration, I struggle up from the soggy ground and wobble off across the tundra towards the distant, rocky pool that is our goal. The padded straps and plastic clips on our dry bags are a boon that Hornby didn't have. Would he say that we're cheating, or just smile and ask to borrow our packs? Something tells me the former response would be more in character. Hornby revelled in difficulty. He once wrote to a friend, *"Hardships are preferable to ease."* While completing Pike's Portage, the steel keel of his fifth canoe of the day resting on his shoulder, and blood from his flayed back staining his shirt, he rebuked a concerned companion, *"Nothing can hurt you if you don't think about it."* I think I understand what he was driving at, but to me, pain avoidance is the best line of defence.

Chris hauled in two more trout today. They're not enough for a full meal, so we save the fillets and instead prepare a savoury concoction of instant rice, cheddar cheese and salami. We call this the rice meal. Good, hot and most importantly, all we can eat.

While dinner is cooking, I start a fire. We're not burning wood for cooking or warmth, but we sometimes burn our accumulated refuse. This is my particular responsibility, and it's satisfying to meet the challenge of having a blaze above the tree line. There's usually no shortage of tinder; it just takes time and patience to collect the requisite handful of dry, dead twigs from among the scattered clumps of dwarf willow and other small shrubs. Fancying myself an expert, I choose each ingredient carefully, snapping the twigs in two and rolling them in the palms of my hands to assess their dryness. Sometimes, no twigs are available, so we take advantage of these natural combustibles wherever we can.

Evidently, the north still provides career opportunities for those of talent and ambition. It's due to my heroic service in managing all-weather campfires along the Nahanni River two years ago that I earned the title "Fire Boy" and won a promotion to garbage control officer for this trip. It's an important assignment. Though a small and mobile society, we generate a varied and constant stream of waste. Today, I incinerate a plastic corn syrup bottle, several slimy Ziploc bags (along with their unrecognizable, fermenting contents), and an unexplained collection of (unused) tampons soaked in Muskol. Tact and discretion are the soul of the serving class, and a wise garbage control officer doesn't ask too many questions. I simply throw these special offerings on the fire along with the rest. Watching the neatly packaged, repellent-soaked fire logs turn to ashes, I muse that someday, someone may try to sell such a product. I speculate on what it might be called (Tampol?) and try to imagine a marketing campaign.

We're now camped about three kilometres upriver from Aylmer Lake. Loons howl mournfully somewhere out near the horizon, and we witness another beautiful, protracted sunset. And so, to bed, at 10:40 p.m., under clear skies and a light breeze, with the temperature falling from 60°F.

Camp Location: 64° 19.41'N 108° 41.27'W
Distance Today: 37 km. paddle, 0.8 km. portage
Distance to Date: 677 km. paddle, 13.1 km. portage

July 26

    A hard day, but light in terms of distance covered, only about 16 kilometres all told. Our "river" is a chain of small, oval-shaped ponds connected by narrow, rock-choked spillways that have to be portaged. Sometimes, even the ponds have rocky barriers blocking our passage. Our "Naturalist's Guide to the Arctic" calls this "deranged drainage," presumably in acknowledgment of the breed of paddlers it attracts. The book assures us that over the course of the next 100,000 years or so, the forces of erosion will prevail, yielding gentle, well-ordered streams. Unfortunately, we can't wait that long. More rock-scouring of our canoe bottoms is a result. Besides dragging the boats and cautiously negotiating the shallow waters, we completed 5 or 6 portages, from 10 to 1000 metres long, over terrain ranging from wet, slippery rocks to dry, level grassland. We reached tonight's camp, on an island near a peninsula in central Savannah Lake, at 7:30 p.m., exactly 11½ hours after we started.
    The area we traversed today was well-populated with wildlife. We saw several young caribou, as well as the tracks and leavings of many others. A snowy owl, yellow-billed loons, assorted gulls, a few parasitic jaegers, and some small flocks of nesting ptarmigans complete the list of today's sightings. We had ringside seats for an attack by a large jaeger on two seagulls. Jaegers get some of their food by intimidating gulls into regurgitating what they have already swallowed. The jaegers then swoop down and catch this pre-digested prize before it even hits the ground: nature's version of income tax.
    Tonight, we enjoy an all-you-can-eat, pan-fried pizza dinner, topped off by seemingly unlimited portions of no-bake cheesecake. Food preparation isn't my department, so I can't

describe how this dessert is created except that it involves adding powder to a water-filled plastic bottle and shaking it vigorously for several minutes. The resulting cold, yellowish mixture is poured onto a bed of pressed graham cracker crumbs and allowed to congeal. Bon appétit! But it tastes much better than it sounds, especially when we're hungry enough to eat just about anything. I hasten to add that I have no complaints about the quality or quantity of our daily bread. The menu is varied and well-planned, and although I'm mildly hungry most of the time and ravenous at meal times, these are certainly not starvation rations. All told, we have over 500 pounds of food at our disposal, including the provisions we picked up at Vodka Lake and another planned resupply at Lupin Mine, up on Contwoyto Lake.

I'm certainly not wasting away, but I do think a lot about food these days. It's a preoccupation shared by my paddling partners and by many other tundra transients over the years. Again, I defer to John Hornby. Who better to address the subject than one who starved to death up here? During a trip to the barrens in 1924, he and his partner Critchell-Bullock flirted with starvation, but survived the experience. In the absence of a real meal, Hornby amused himself and his companion by describing the following imaginary feast:

The wines first, Bullock. We should have a magnum of the best champagne – Mumm's or Heidsieck. And a bottle of Old Brown Sherry. Now for the dinner. I'll order carefully. Norwegian anchovies in pure olive oil, chopped up and spread on thin toast. And soup? I think the clear green turtle will do. Then sweet bread patties or a small lobster thermidor. Gad, can't you taste that lobster? There's no choice for the next of course. It must be roast pheasant, royally stuffed, served with slightly salted shoestring potatoes. A little salad of crisp watercress with Roquefort dressing. Then for dessert a choice. Mince pies, assorted crystallized fruits, sponge fingers, brick ice cream, Stilton and Camembert with crackers, assorted nuts and Turkish coffee.

Those travellers having the luxury of actually consuming their favourite personal fuel have left behind a legacy of menus as varied as the personalities and proclivities of those who enjoyed them. For R.M. Patterson, whose journal, "The Dangerous River," is a favourite of mine, true gastronomic bliss was achieved beside the Nahanni River, early on a summer morning in 1927. As the sun's first rays appeared over the canyon rim below Virginia Falls and the mist from this awesome cataract wafted gently past his camp, Patterson breakfasted on porridge, fresh mountain goat liver, bacon, buttered bannock, marmalade and tea, topped off with a bowl of wild raspberries in cream. No Pop-Tarts need apply. Other comfort foods appear more plebeian, but were doubtless at least as satisfying to those who consumed them. For the map maker Guy Blanchet, heading homeward along Great Slave Lake in 1924, nothing was finer than to dine on *"prunes, porridge, bannock and beans"* to relieve the monotony of his summer-long diet of caribou meat. For Warburton Pike, luxury for *"a man in the wilds"* consisted of *"... flour, bacon, tea, tobacco, sugar, a packet of letters from England and a bottle of brandy..."* For King Beaulieu, who accompanied Pike to the barrens in the early 1890s, a simple thing like bread and butter provided the greatest pleasure. As he explained beside some northern campfire, *"Ah Monsieur, une fois j'ai goûté le pain avec le beurre; le bon Dieu a fait ces deux choses-là exprès pour manger ensemble."*

As for me, I would never consider inflicting my simple camp remedies for hunger on either friends or strangers. Calories and convenience are at the top of my personal hierarchy of culinary essentials, far outweighing such trivial factors as flavour, texture and presentation; this is the main reason I'm stuck washing dishes and burning garbage. But I do know that, like an army, adventure marches on its stomach. Excuse me while I pull out a chunk of Baker's chocolate I've been saving...

Speaking of personal hierarchies, sleeping comes a close second to eating on our current list of priorities. My own bedtime routine is well-established by now. First, I spritz lens cleaner on my dirty glasses. Then it's time to update the journal, which usually takes about an hour, most of it spent with the blunt end of the pencil in my mouth. Next, I bandage any scrapes or cracks on my hands and apply moleskin to any impending blisters on my feet. I then rub my hands with lanolin. I hate the mess and the misleading, yellowish stains inside my sleeping bag, but the hand cream prevents the chapping and cracking that would otherwise result from daily immersion in cold water. We each have our own personal supply. It doesn't get truly dark at night, so I cover my eyes with a pair of blinders, obtained on a British Airways flight from London to Johannesburg a few years ago. All this geriatric, bedtime fuss is an inconvenience, but it helps ensure a good rest and a fully operational body the next morning, so it's worth the effort. Our ambitious schedule doesn't make any allowances for malfunctioning parts. The same principle of preventative maintenance applies to the boats; this evening, Chris applied cold-cure resin to some of the deeper scratches on the canoe bottoms, where the Kevlar cloth was becoming exposed.

It was sunny again today, with a high temperature of about 70°F. If the weather doesn't become more arctic-like soon, we may run out of sunscreen. To bed at 10:30 p.m. on this fine, clear evening.

Camp Location: 64° 25.17'N 108° 56.44'W
Distance Today: 16 km. paddle, 3 km. portage
Distance to Date: 693 km. paddle, 16.1 km. portage

Chapter 11: FORREST GUMP AND GATORADE

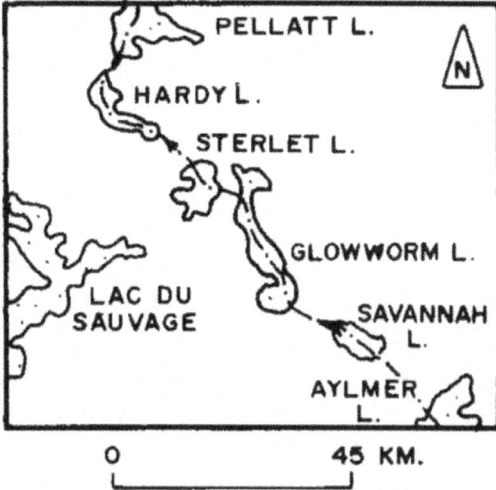

July 27

Another day of little paddles and little portages, five of the latter, I think. The wind picked up during the afternoon, so portaging the 55-pound, 18½-foot canoes became much more of a challenge. Under these conditions, our watercraft could easily become Kevlar kites if hoisted onto our shoulders during a strong gust. The boats are extremely difficult to carry in a straight line during these winds, which tug on the bow or stern, and push against the gunnels, exerting a painful, energy-draining torque on knees, waists and shoulders. So, we resort to the tandem portage method, as practiced by Chris and Myrna last summer. Each canoe is shouldered by one person while the other, heavily laden with a pack, holds a short rope tied to the stern and acts as a rudder. We refer to this colloquially as the "dog and pony show." Imagine a bobbing, inverted canoe, driven across the tundra by a pair of anonymous legs, dragging behind it a heavily laden, slowly trudging human, head bowed as if being led into captivity. Peculiar imagery aside, it's a method that works well and is essential for portaging a long, light canoe across the wind-blown tundra. It's also a feat of coordination and teamwork, not easily mastered. More than once, I've yelled at Jill to "Hold it steady!" not realizing that she had fallen to the ground 50 yards back and was struggling to get herself and her 100-pound pack upright again. At other times, I've almost speared her with the stern by stopping suddenly or swerving to avoid a rock or hummock.

Tandem or solo, I can't say I enjoy portaging much, or even tolerate it with good humour. The strong language I learned while working as a geological assistant in northern Manitoba is often used, directed at the canoe, the wind, the hummocks, the boulders, or the muskeg. For the most part, it's uttered under my breath, but I'm sure I've been overheard as my mutters swirl and echo under my long, yellow cap of Kevlar. Today, as we plod wearily along, I'm struck by two thoughts: first, that I have never before set foot on this particular piece of ground and second, that I will never again set foot on this particular piece of ground. In the heat of battle in the midst of a long portage, I can't say which idea is more satisfying.

But now the day's work is done and I'm perched high above the distant camp on an esker, a narrow, sinuous ridge of gravel and sand deposited, we are told, by meltwater flowing beneath a receding glacier. Method of formation aside, it's no great mystery to me why God created eskers. They're here so yuppie canoeists from the south can perch high above the tundra and relax in the cool, bug-free breeze. I'm parked up here on my Therm-a-Rest throne, living la dolce vita and admiring the view. To my right, the sun settles low, glinting and sparkling on a multitude of small lakes. To my left, the moon is a ghostly sphere in the pale, silver-blue sky. The tents are tiny, blue-and-yellow mushrooms, and the canoes are flecks of yellow on the adjacent shore. I can see for miles up here, a seemingly endless vista of gently undulating tundra, a green-tinged ocean, frozen in time. Immersed in our daily urban routines, we don't often experience the power of a far perspective. Instead, we're usually focused on the foreground, solving the latest problem, interacting with screens, books, keyboards and signs. As I scan the expansive scene in front of me, I can feel my eyeballs relax and elongate as they focus on infinity.

We conquered another 11 hard-fought kilometres today. In the most recent of his periodic state-of-the-expedition speeches, Chris reported that all is going according to plan and that our current rate of progress will get us to the Arctic Ocean by summer's end. I'm starting to believe we might pull this thing off and that I'm up to the challenge. During our initial portages, I wasn't so sure. The intensity and duration of the punishing, physical labour took me by surprise, and I was convinced that I was the only one suffering. Everyone else acted so incomprehensibly cheery, even when bent under the weight of an impossibly heavy load. I see now that we all suffer; it's just that some of us are better at hiding it than others. I remember with shame my relief, even joy, when I first heard one of my companions describe their physical discomfort in no uncertain terms, for it meant that I wasn't alone, not only one who might crack. Struggling on an equal footing with others makes the whole enterprise seem more equitable and more bearable. In other words, misery really does love company.

Off to bed at 9:45 p.m. this fair evening, after yet another warm and sunny day.

Camp Location: 64° 32.21'N 108° 59.19'W
Distance Today: 11 km. paddle, 3.3 km. portage
Distance to Date: 704 km. paddle, 19.4 km. portage

July 28

Two more portages today and then a hard, northward struggle up Glowworm Lake into the teeth of a strong headwind. Lots of bobbing, bouncing and smacking of hulls as we battered our way northward. We're now camped on a small peninsula about seven kilometres south of the next portage that will lead us towards Sterlet Lake.

The swell today was high, and spray skirts were the order of the day. Despite the fabric decking, water still tends to gain entry via the cockpits, and Chris and Christy had to bail out their boat a couple of times. I had my usual problem with water leaking in around the Velcro fastenings where I sit. No harm done, just some damp clothing that quickly dried in the wind.

After supper, I walk away from camp again to experience the addictive solitude of the barrens. Some say it can drive a person crazy, but tonight it's medicine: a brief, necessary escape from our tiny, intense society that sometimes generates its own brand of insanity. Within minutes, I'm immersed in a seeming infinity of land and sky. In the foreground, the diminutive leaves of ground-hugging dwarf willows rustle in the breeze, back-lit by a low but persistent sun. Angular, lichen-stained boulders send their long, irregular shadows over patches of gently waving cotton grass. Small songbirds flit about silently at knee height, as if their wings have been clipped and their summer music has already been sung. Interwoven caribou tracks and trails mark the ground in braided patterns, recording generations of instinct-driven motion. Behind it all, silence lurks like a solid force, waiting to replace the soothing voice of the soft wind. These various bits and pieces of the surrounding landscape can be easily documented; the same can't be said of the environment they comprise, or the emotions they invoke. As the aristocratic adventurer David T. Hanbury confessed upon first viewing the tundra in 1899, *"Its charm and the sense of freedom it gives are very impressive, but cannot be described."* I sit on the ground with my back against a boulder. Strangely, I feel at home in these alien surroundings. If I closed my eyes, I would soon be asleep. Bone weary, I imagine yielding to this temptation and sleeping a blissful, enchanted sleep until the end of time. But if I did that, who would burn the garbage and carry the canoe? Always the pragmatist, I struggle to my feet and head back to camp.

Clear skies remained with us today, along with a stiff wind and scattered clouds. Earlier in the day, when the wind blew from the southwest, we smelt the smoke of a distant forest fire, somewhere below the tree line.

Camp Location: 64° 38.71'N 109° 16.84'W
Distance Today: 19 km. paddle, 2.0 km. portage
Distance to Date: 723 km. paddle, 21.4 km. portage

July 29

More paddling. More portaging. Have I ever done anything else? Will I ever do anything else? I used to live for Fridays. Now I don't even know what day it is. Who cares? Whatever the day, it'll mean more paddling, more portaging. We do the latter by double tripping, meaning we each take one load over, walk back again feeling lighter than feathers, and then repeat step one, with a little less energy. Once we've each made our two trips, everything is packed into the canoes again, and we're able to move on.

At the start of today's first portage, Christy encases her right leg in a formidable-looking, elastic and steel brace, the fruit of a skiing accident and subsequent knee surgery. It appears that the heavy loads and uneven terrain are beginning to have an impact. Full of his usual sympathy, Chris calls out, "Run, Forrest! Run!" in an oblique reference to a scene early in the movie, "Forrest Gump." Christy just smiles, hoists her pack, and sets out across the boulders and hummocks. As she herself said a few days ago, "There are no wimps on this trip." That's a debatable thesis, but her saying it out loud was good for morale.

Back in our boats, conversation is less frequent these days. Each of us lost in our own thoughts, we hear only the wind and the rhythmic swish and gurgle of blades cutting through the transparent water, punctuated by the random thump of paddle shafts against gunnels. On occasion, loons, terns or gulls keep us company with their various cries, seemingly of welcome, but probably warning us to stay away from their nests. Sometimes the merging bird calls bring to mind the distant cheering of a large crowd. Chris then stands up in the stern of his boat and raises his arms, acknowledging the attention of an imaginary fan club, which he says has chartered a plane and flown in to watch him pass.

The morning's light winds give way to a dead calm, which, along with the bright sunshine, makes for hot work. But I'm not complaining. It's much better than paddling into a strong wind, and it's okay to sweat because we have ready access to all the cold water we could possibly use. We just scoop it up in our plastic mugs and drink our fill. Up here, the idea of carrying drinking water on a canoe trip is as ludicrous as the notion of carrying a box of sand through the Sahara. The number of lakes and ponds full of pure, fresh water is incredible, most of them unnamed and unremarked, seldom involved in the schemes of men.

Today as I paddle, I tilt my head and examine the surface of the cold liquid as it slides by at about six kilometres to the hour. I try to note and account for the subtle variations in its colour. Where the water is deepest, it's a dark, blue-black, almost the colour of ripe blueberries. When we enter shallower water, the colour changes to a pale, tropical turquoise, reminiscent of Gatorade, or a certain blue-flavoured Popsicle I used to enjoy. As the depth decreases even further, the water becomes transparent, and the red, yellow, black, cream, and brown colours of the underlying rocks dominate, like the colours of a well-constructed ice cream sundae. When the depth decreases yet again, we grind over a rock, and I'm jolted from my food fantasy in time to help avoid the next collision.

Paddling into the rock gardens of the shallows, one can empathize with a pilot, who, lost and low on fuel, descends through the clouds and is confronted with mountain peaks left, right and centre. But while the pilot has the option of pulling back on the stick and gaining altitude, we're stuck working with only two dimensions. When all else fails, we're out of the boats and pulling them along, ready to hop back in when we reach deeper water.

Perhaps the worst part of paddling brittle envelopes of resin and Kevlar through the barrens is negotiating the transition between lake and land at the start of each portage. It's here that we experience most of the bumping and grinding. Many of the "landings" are merely ill-defined zones of rocky water. We often find ourselves balancing heavy packs on wobbling gunnels, while standing on slippery boulders, knee-deep in cold water. No broken necks yet, just damp clothing when we slide unintentionally, or step intentionally into deeper water to cushion the boat or secure our luggage. As the canoe lightens, it can be pulled closer to shore. Once empty, it can be lifted out of the water, and the portage can begin.

Despite the hard work, there's comfort in the familiar routine. While Jill clips various loose articles to the outside of the three largest packs, I prepare the canoe by lashing our carbon fibre paddles to the cross-pieces using two small bungee cords. A cotter pin is then pulled from the slider of the rear seat and inserted into the "pogo stick," a piece of spring-loaded, vertical aluminum tubing connecting the thwart to the keel. The pogo stick is designed to flex and absorb impacts that would otherwise damage the hull. Inserting the pin locks it in place so the canoe doesn't bounce around too much during the portage. Next, I tie my life jacket to the canoe behind the rear seat, along with a spare fishing rod, to provide a few degrees of trim; it's best to be stern-heavy and bow-high so I can see where I'm going. Finally, I don my small daypack, and then hoist the canoe to my thighs, pausing for two heartbeats before swinging it up onto my back so that the thwart rests more or less comfortably in the crevice between my shoulders and the top of the pack. D'accord! Allons-y!

Repetition has led to improvement, but what little portaging ability we've developed so far can't match the skills of the voyageurs of old, who reportedly juggled their heavy boats and bulky baggage with contemptuous ease. All things considered though, their presence on a long trip was probably a mixed blessing. Sure, they carried bone-crushing, 300-pound packs without a murmur and serenaded their companions with "La Claire Fontaine" for 14 hours a day, but according to Dr. Richardson of Franklin's 1821 expedition, they each expected *"...8 pounds of solid meat as their customary daily allowance."* Our payload is less than 300 pounds, and we don't have the fancy sound system (leaving aside the repetitive strains of Chris's "cowboy song"), but we're also getting much better mileage. All told, we're only consuming about 2½ pounds of food per person per day by my reckoning. We don't have to waste precious time hunting caribou and roasting chunks of raw, bloody meat over smoky flames. Just give us a few platefuls of lake trout or pasta and a piece of chocolate, and we're good to go.

We're now north of Sterlet Lake and just a few short hops away from Hardy Lake, from which we will hop to Pellatt Lake, from which we will hop to Contwoyto Lake, and then make a long run up to Lupin Mine, where our next resupply is waiting. Our packs are getting lighter, and we could always use more exercise.

It's 11 p.m. and time for bed. An 8 a.m. start is scheduled for tomorrow.

Camp Location: 64° 46.78'N 109° 42.10'W
Distance Today: 29 km. paddle, 2.2 km. portage
Distance to Date: 752 km. paddle, 23.6 km. portage

Performing some routine systems maintenance.

Christy struts her stuff on a long, rocky portage.

The dog and pony show: Jill and her canoe march across the tundra (Chris Morris).

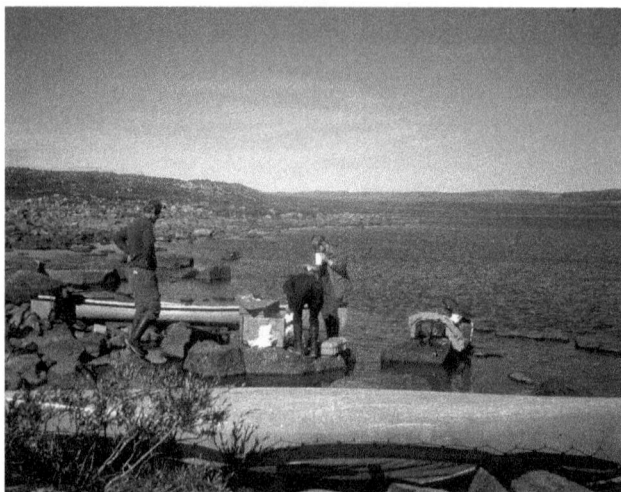

Breakfast at a rocky landing.

Chapter 12: FREE LOVE ON PELLATT LAKE

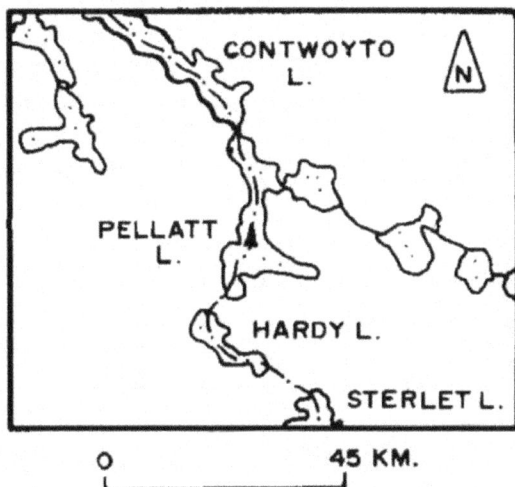

July 30

It's 2 p.m. and we're windbound about halfway up Hardy Lake. The gusts we fought in getting here were almost strong enough to stop us dead in our tracks. Forward progress was reduced to a shoulder-straining crawl of about two and a half kilometres per hour. Waves hammered against the bows of the boats, and the wind snatched and plucked at our lightweight paddles, making forward motion through the air almost as much work as backwards motion through the water. So, we're holed up on an island until conditions improve. If necessary, we'll do an overnight paddle, our first since Artillery Lake. We had a short, sharp shower and a bit of thunder this morning just before the wind picked up. Chris and I were carrying the canoes at the time and kept mostly dry. The women, trapped in the harnesses of their bulky packs, enjoyed a cleansing shower, a gift from nature's bounty.

Last night, I had another in a series of vivid, recurring dreams. I am in a large, ornate boardroom, making a presentation to a group of important clients. I have lost their attention and their respect. They nudge one another and snicker, making scathing comments under their breath. I wake up sweating. I believe it's a sign that the accumulated mental toxins generated by 14 continuous years of employment-generated anxiety are gradually leaching from my system. Despite the hard, physical work ahead, the relief of waking up and finding that I'm up here on the tundra is inexpressible and sublime.

The wind continues into the late afternoon. I try blueberry picking to help fill my stomach and pass the time. Half an hour of stooping labour yields only a small handful of fruit, so I give it up. The berries are low and scattered; any serious attempt at a harvest would require a vacuum cleaner with a very long cord.

This evening, the wind finally drops, and we leave our temporary camp around 7:15 p.m., paddling in relative calm until about 10:30, when we stop for the night near the south end of Pellatt Lake. Extremely buggy. A quick cup of chicken noodle soup and then to bed.

Camp Location: 64° 57.01'N 109° 44.54'W
Distance Today: 24 km. paddle, 2 km. portage
Distance to Date: 776 km. paddle, 25.6 km. portage

July 31

Today's travel starts at around 9 a.m., an hour later than usual. Jill and I struggle to get our boat back into the water among all the rocks. We can't remember how we managed last night's unloading in a foggy haze of insects and fatigue.

We pry our weary way northward up the centre of Pellatt Lake in the calm heat, still plagued by bugs. Today's variety are roughly the size and shape of black flies, but apparently without the sharp teeth, or whatever black flies use to deliver their injurious afflictions. They sit on top of the mirror-flat water, supported by surface tension and rise in excited clouds as our canoes slice through their midst. It seems we're the big yellow taxis they've been waiting for. They swarm aboard, clogging our eyes, ears and noses. We choke on them if we dare to mouth breathe. They coat our clothing and every available surface of the canoes. Some flit from place to place. Others crawl hurriedly across the baggage as if on urgent business. Still others couple, writhe, wriggle, and flop. I'm no entomologist, but I know reproduction when viewed at close range. It's sex in a canoe, and we're witnessing the chaotic consequences of free love, a cautionary tale from nature.

We are near the north end of Pellatt Lake by about 4 p.m., and a line of dark thunderheads rises ahead of us. A north wind builds, dispersing the mobile orgy. Soon, we recognize part of the winter road that connects Lupin Mine with Yellowknife. A seasonal passage, it's constructed mostly of snow and ice. In summer, only the raised, gravel roadbed between the lakes is discernible, and it's a road to nowhere, but it does have the makings of an excellent portage route to Contwoyto Lake. As we get closer, we notice large clouds of dust rising from the road's surface on a height of land about two kilometres away. It looks like a moving vehicle. How can that be? Moments later, we realize that the dust is being blasted from the road by a violent, rapidly approaching squall. The first gusts arrive about 2 minutes later and accelerate into the strongest winds we've faced this summer, forcing us to make an emergency run for shore.

So, we're windbound once again. For now, we've escaped the rain, but dark clouds and thunder fill the sky to the north and west. Determined to make the most of our unanticipated but welcome rest, we lounge on the tundra and watch the whitecaps, while dining on smoked oysters, cheese, raisins, peanuts and Belgian chocolate, a civilized meal for the middle of nowhere in a gale. Adding to the festive atmosphere, Christy digs out a large bag of gummy bears, those infamous gumdrops shaped like Winnie-the-Pooh, that have helped put so many dentists' children through university.

After the meal, my rumbling stomach still rivals the

growling thunder. Unwilling to miss any opportunity to absorb calories, I head inland on another quest for blueberries. This time, the harvest is more successful, and I'm almost able to eat my fill, grazing through the low-lying bushes on my hands and knees like a cow let out to pasture. When I return to the others, Chris approaches me with a steaming cup of hot chocolate. Falling to his knees, he holds it up, cradled in his two hands as though offering me nectar from the gods. Judging by his broad, impish grin, he has probably spiked it with something noxious. I sniff at it suspiciously, but the rich, chocolate odour overpowers caution and I drink it all down, with no ill effects.

The wind refuses to die, so we make this our camp of record for the evening. To help pass the time, I decide to appoint myself the official poet laureate of the expedition. My first challenge in this new capacity will be to capture Chris's unique outlook on life in rhyme. It's a tough assignment. But then I remember a suitable ballad I read long ago in National Lampoon magazine, so I plagiarize it and recite it to the others as my own. It's called "A Pack of Wild Dogs" and I repeat it now:

A pack of wild dogs,
A pack of wild dogs,
A pack of wild dogs are we.
We roam the hills,
Bereft of job skills,
And we don't care where we pee.

Chris is delighted with this poetic observation. The women are more muted in their enthusiasm, but in the end, the decision to call ourselves the Wild Dogs Canoe Club is unanimous. Our motto, inscribed on a new set of custom-made, half-litre coffee mugs, will be "P ubi non curamus." Outsiders will think the "P" stands for paddle, but we insiders will know the truth.

Camp Location: 65° 11.50'N 109° 44.00'W

Free Love on Pellatt Lake

Distance Today: 28 km. paddle, 0 km. portage
Distance to Date: 804 km. paddle, 25.6 km. portage

August 1

Heavy rain commences at about 4 a.m. and last night's strong winds continue. We decide to delay our planned 7 a.m. departure for a couple of hours. The wind is still blowing hard when we break camp at 9 a.m., and loading each canoe is like trying to put saddlebags on a bucking horse. One person wrestles with the boat to keep it from battering itself to death on the sharp rocks as the other heaves in the baggage, wedges it into position, and fastens down the skirt.

There are only a few kilometres to paddle before we reach the head of Pellatt Lake and the start of our well-constructed portage. Fronted by a gravel beach on a windward shore, it's an easy landing. Various scraps of lumber are scattered on the beach along with the remains of several long, wooden boxes designed to hold drill core samples.

Our burdens don't feel any lighter. Still, it's a pleasure to march down the centre of a hard-packed, gravel roadway instead of stumbling over hummocks, wading through bogs or hopping from boulder to boulder. There's a time in mid-portage when no lake is visible, and we seem to be walking our canoes and packs along a waterless prairie back road, like latter-day Noahs in search of a flood. Eventually, we come upon a stack of culverts and metal drums, and 100 metres later, reach the south end of Contwoyto Lake. A sign on the shoulder of the gravel road proclaims, "Lupin Mine 100 kilometres." So now we know the exact distance to our next resupply.

Exploring the lake shore before heading back for our second loads, we discover a three-wheeled, all-terrain vehicle with the key in the ignition and gas in the tank. Chris and Christy are the first to make this find, and they swarm over the big, motorized tricycle, hoping to start it up and mechanize the remainder of our portage. Jill and I join in, spouting random ignorance, spiced with words such as fuel valves, kill switches and spark plugs. We never once consider the morality of unauthorized borrowing. We probably would have left a note with cash to cover the cost of the fuel, but it's a moot point. Despite (or perhaps because of) the seven university degrees collectively behind us, we can't make it go. Reluctantly, we plod the two kilometres back to Pellatt to begin the second carry. By the time we've each walked the required six kilometres, it's time for a breakfast of pancakes and maple syrup. While eating, I wander along the Contwoyto shoreline and discover several five-gallon plastic jerrycans full of gasoline. There's also a small marker and cairn placed by the Northwest Territories Department of Natural Resources indicating the future border of the new territory of Nunavut, soon to be carved from the Northwest Territories.

We load up and shove off, heading northward on Contwoyto, wary of a crosswind blowing hard from the east. Shortly after our launch, there's a loud, rhythmic thumping from behind. Before we can swivel our heads to take a look, a small, brightly coloured Hughes 500 helicopter skims over us at an altitude of about 200 feet, banking to give its passengers a better look at the scruffy occupants of the twin, yellow canoes, pitching and rolling in the lumpy, grey water. A brief wave from the pilot and it's gone, off towards the northeast.

After several hours spent battling swell and crosswinds, and dodging in and out from behind a chain of small islands along the western shore of this very large lake, we make our camp on an island about 30 kilometres northwest of our last portage. It's an interesting spot: a large, irregularly shaped mound of sand, bordered by a series of linear sand spits and beaches. Many islands in this part of the lake are of similar construction, with sand spits oriented in the same north-south configuration, as if they once formed part of a continuous esker, now partly inundated by the lake.

There's a continuing threat of rain this evening, so we inhabit the cook tent. Dinner tonight is the rice meal. For dessert, there's a bowl of chocolate pudding each. It all goes down very well. Later, I make a casual comment about finding a cigarette butt during our last portage. This sets Chris off on a nicotine craving. He knows I carry a bit of cash and guesses there may be smokes for sale at Lupin Mine, so he asks to borrow money from me at any terms I choose to name. It's tempting to take advantage of this situation, but I believe it's in everyone's best interest to keep our leader happy, so I promise to buy him a pack of his favourite brand. Chris is immensely pleased and declares that he's "morally indebted" to me. Apparently, that's how a philosopher says thanks. I'll bank my newly acquired moral capital, so it's available to cover any future transgressions.

Camp Location: 65° 23.36'N 110° 13.67'W
Distance Today: 32 km. paddle, 2 km. portage
Distance to Date: 836 km. paddle, 27.6 km. portage

Chapter 13: STRIKING GOLD AT LUPIN

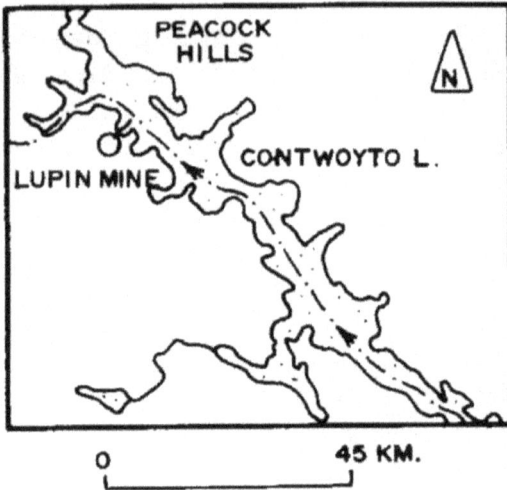

August 2

Through waves to Lupin we did batter,
To make our flaccid food bags fatter,
In hopes Contwoyto would become,
As flat as p*** upon a platter.

    Contwoyto is anything but flat, but we press on anyway, pitching and rolling our way northwest, reaching Lupin Mine after 15 hours and 68 hard-fought kilometres. We hear it first: a low, barely audible hum that tickles our ears like the lazy drone of a distant aircraft. But planes in flight generally move. This noise is of constant pitch and direction, and we realize it's the faint sound of massive ventilators, borne to us intermittently on the wind. Later, from a distance of about 12 kilometres, we notice an incongruous, orange rectangle on the distant horizon with a vertical headframe jutting above. In this landscape, smooth edges and regular geometric shapes are easy to spot, especially when they're the colour of a ripe pumpkin.

At 10 p.m., seven kilometres out, we come upon two diehard miners-turned-fishermen in one of the recreational boats owned by Echo Bay Mines. It's a green-painted, aluminum outboard called the "Sham-Rock." It's obvious that we're not local, so they motor over to check us out. Within 30 seconds, Chris has bummed two cigarettes and is puffing contentedly, the shreds of tobacco and my moral capital both going up in smoke. We chat with the miners as our boats bob side-by-side in the choppy water. When we ask them if they think it would be okay to camp near the company dock, we're told, "Sure, if you really want to, but wouldn't you rather have a hot meal, shower and bed?" With those tantalizing possibilities in front of us, tired muscles are forgotten, and our planned caffeine break on a nearby peninsula is cancelled. We push on towards the lights of the mine, which have now taken on a new significance. The occupants of the Sham-Rock offer to tow us, but that would be a risky undertaking, especially in this swell, and anyway, our ropes are all stowed away, so we decline their well-intentioned offer. They tell us they'll inform "security" of our impending arrival and roar away northward, hull booming rhythmically as it strikes the waves.

A quarter hour later, during our final, highly motivated sprint towards Lupin, a second vessel approaches us and throttles down. This southbound, aluminum-hulled outboard carries an Inuit family. They're curious about our origin and destination, so we tell them about our route. The head of the family assumes we're aiming for the Burnside River and is surprised that we're making for the Hood. "Lots of portages," he says succinctly. (I groan inwardly.) They tell us they have a tent camp down the lake. From our discreet inquiries, we learn that they're the owners of the all-terrain vehicle we had tried to commandeer. We describe what we saw, but are tactful enough to avoid mentioning our attempted piracy. Curiosity satisfied, the man at the helm twists the throttle of his black, 30-horsepower Mercury outboard, and the boat continues southward. We return to our paddles on an opposite course, minds spinning from these sudden, successive contacts with technologically advanced, waterborne tribes. At least they're friendly.

At 10:30 p.m., with most of our energy reserves expended, we enter a small bay, turn left, and make a last dash for a cluster of lights near the shoreline. The mine complex itself is set on a low hill about a kilometre inland. Along with the relief of achieving our goal, there's apprehension. Did the miners have the right to extend such a generous invitation? How will the "security" they spoke of react to our arrival? Do we still have enough energy left to build our camp if necessary? Christy remarks on the complex's sinister appearance. Illuminated in the harsh glare of a constellation of white and orange floodlights, it resembles an isolated Siberian gulag awaiting its next group of prisoners. As we approach an imposing barrier of large boulders, vehicle headlights shine in our faces, and a voice penetrates the gloom. "Follow the breakwater around to the opening!" This we do, and glide into the calm water of a small harbour. We beach our hulls on the pea-sized gravel and stumble ashore. Ted, a former military man, now a security officer for Echo Bay Mines, watches our arrival. The miners' call got him out of bed, but he's on call 24 hours a day during his two-week shift, so he doesn't seem to resent the intrusion: "At least you didn't get here at 3 a.m."

He tells us to put ourselves and our gear in his van. A big, self-propelled box on wheels; what a useful invention! The motor's running, so we move quickly on rubbery legs, inverting our canoes on the gravel beach before gathering our personal belongings and food packs and hoisting them into the vehicle. Minutes later, we're blinking under rows of fluorescent lights as we clump down the solid hallways of the mine's well-equipped recreational and living complex, sweating in the unaccustomed warmth, and reeling from extended exposure to the motion of the lake. Instead of a cell block, Ted shows us to our assigned rooms: private, individual rooms no less, each with its own bathroom and shower. Welcome to paradise! But as tired as we are, sleep can wait, because another wonder is revealed: a late evening meal is being served in the dining hall:

veal, roast potatoes, vegetables, warm fresh bread, fruit punch, cherry pie (my favourite!), root beer-flavoured ice cream, etc., all we can eat, no payment required. We load up our trays with hasty gratitude. Ted then directs us to a comfortable lounge in front of a big-screen TV, blaring out the theme song for "Married with Children." As the Beatles once sang, it's all too much! To bed at 1 a.m., stuffed to contentment, and totally spent.

Camp Location: 65° 45.80'N 111° 13.75'W
Distance Today: 68 km. paddle, 0 km. portage
Distance to Date: 904 km. paddle, 27.6 km. portage

August 3

After a deep, dreamless sleep, I'm up at 6:30 by force of habit and immediately head to the dining hall for a huge breakfast of sausages, scrambled eggs, and pancakes. I join Chris and Ted there, but the women have chosen sleep over food; either choice is reasonable, I have to admit. Breakfast ends at 7, so I take four extra Danishes for them, but my stomach is bigger than my heart. I nibble at the edges of the round pastries until they begin to resemble a set of old tires gnawed by rats. Chris suggests it would be cruel to offer Jill and Christy such poor fare, so together we finish what the rats started. After breakfast, I visit the laundromat, throwing everything into the wash except what I'm wearing.

Once we're all up and active, we go to the baggage room where our next re-supply is waiting. We spend the rest of the morning reorganizing our packs to absorb this bounty. The bannock mixes have gone mouldy, but Chris activates the silky side of his personality and is able to charm 78 cups of flour and some baking soda from the kitchen staff. We soon recreate the required recipes. We're also given an unexpected bonus, a four-litre container of naphtha abandoned here last year by another canoeist. Ted locates this in a warehouse and hands it over. This greatly extends our fuel supply and will allow us to enjoy hot drinks more often.

It's 48 ° F outside, with strong winds and heavy rain. After postponing our departure several times and consulting with the mine's weather office, Chris officially declares the expedition windbound for the day. No one argues with this decision; some of us were counting on it.

Ted has us each sign a sheet of paper and write down our home addresses. He then gives us the run of the complex, checking back with us occasionally. The rest of this now lazy day is spent reading, napping, eating, shopping at the mine's small variety store, and talking with off-duty miners. Christy finds one miner who got arrested for drunk driving in her hometown of Hawkesbury. Small world.

Later, we're able to enjoy the Olympic Games on the big-screen TV, live from Atlanta and are pleased to see Canada's 4 x 100 metre relay team win a gold medal. I have a sudden flashback to a hotel room in Cochrane, Ontario, where I watched Canada's Ben Johnson "win" a gold medal in the 100 metre sprints in Barcelona, only to lose it again after the post-race drug test. I had just returned from a short camping trip to James Bay with friends Jeff and Heather. The sense of relaxation and warmth close on the heels of rain, cold and hard work is rediscovered today. I hope the disappointing drug tests stay in the past.

In light of Canada's latest Olympic success, it's fitting that we're living at a gold mine. The ore is extracted, refined on-site to a valuable amalgam of silver and gold, and then flown south. We notice an X-ray machine in the baggage room and assume it's to check outgoing luggage for stolen precious metals. Ted corrects this misconception, telling us it's used to check incoming luggage for alcohol. Lupin is a "dry" mine, and prohibition is strictly enforced. "Keeps things a lot quieter," he says.

I learned other things about Lupin today. About 250 miners are here at a time. They work 12-hour daily shifts over a two-week period and then are flown out to Edmonton for a 14-day weekend. Some live there, but we're told others have homes as far away as Nova Scotia. The wages at this non-unionized workplace are high, and the company pays for room and board. Facilities for off-duty miners include movies, satellite TV, pool tables, video games, a weight room, squash courts, a gym, and a marina with fishing boats that can be signed out on a first-come, first-served basis. The company provides the gasoline, and the fishing is excellent. There's also a six-hole golf course, laid out on sand instead of grass. There's a baseball diamond and a travelling team that competes in the "Top of the World Baseball Tournament" at the Polaris Mine on Cornwallis Island, near the north magnetic pole. Employees are allowed to have guests at the mine site, including a free flight from Edmonton and free room and board. They stay in a guest house connected to the rest of the complex by a tunnel. Why didn't my high school career counsellor tell me about all this?

Re-examining our food supply, we find we have more luxury items than will fit into our bulging packs. We offer the surplus to the kitchen, but health regulations forbid them from accepting it. Ted says he'll pass it on to Inuit families in the local area, so we stack it on shelves in the baggage room. It includes corn syrup, raisins, coffee, and chocolate and should be well-received; I know I'd like it. When forced by necessity to pour maple syrup down a drain to make the container available for our expanded fuel supply, I almost cry.

This evening, I review the notes on my well-thumbed, bug-stained maps and realize that 15 kilometres due north of the gold-bearing rocks of Lupin, another treasure lies hidden in the Peacock Hills, on the far side of Contwoyto. It's a legacy of Sir John Franklin's first encounter with this large, long lake, a meeting he did not expect or enjoy:

On the 13th [of September, 1821] *in thick heavy weather we had the extreme mortification to find ourselves on the borders of a large lake which we subsequently learned from the Indians was named Contwoyto or Rum Lake. Neither of its extremities could be seen so we coasted the* [shoreline] *in search of a crossing place. The lake being bounded by steep and lofty hills, our march was very fatiguing...we supped off a single partridge and some tripe de roche. This unpalatable weed was now quite nauseous to the whole party and caused bowel complaints...the men getting weaker every day, it became necessary to lighten their burdens of everything except ammunition, clothing and the instruments required to find our way. I therefore deposited at this encampment many of our instruments.*

If I had a job at Lupin Mine, I'd trade my fishing rod for a metal detector and spend my spare time treasure hunting across the lake.

Camp Location: 65° 45.80'N 111° 13.75'W
Distance Today: 0 km. paddle, 0 km. portage
Distance to Date: 904 km. paddle, 27.6 km. portage

Chapter 14: SURFIN' SAFARI

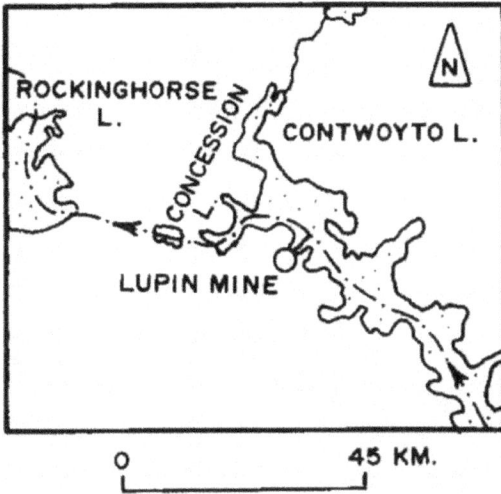

August 4

 The holiday is over, so we're all up at 6 a.m. for breakfast in the cafeteria. The large Canadian flag outside is horizontal, rippling and snapping in the wind. The sky is dark grey. There's no precipitation, but the forecast from the weather office is less than encouraging: wind increasing throughout the day with a chance of rain later. It's already blowing hard from the northeast, so we'll have to fight it head-on to get out of the small bay that shelters the mine. We'll then have to turn left and run broadside to the waves in our heavily loaded canoes for several kilometres before allowing the wind to push us westward into a long, sinuous bay at the northwest corner of the lake.

 At 7 a.m., Ted pulls up outside the baggage room in a dusty, crew-cab pickup truck. We load it with our gear and replenished food packs, and he drives us to the marina. When we arrive, there's not much conversation. The wind is whipping the lake into whitecaps, and waves are beating against the stone breakwater. It's not the best day for waterborne recreation, but there's little choice; we must go on if we're to maintain enough psychological momentum to finish the trip. Another day at Lupin, and we might have gotten too fat and lazy to continue. Already, the biweekly jet service south to Edmonton was becoming a subtle temptation. Now that we're back at our boats, we've each recommitted ourselves to the task at hand, tacitly accepting the fine print in the contract, the clause about having too much distance to cover to confine our paddling to calm weather. It's a truth we've lived by for over 900 kilometres, so far.

Ted stands by while we load the canoes, taking extra care to fasten the spray skirts securely. A quick handshake and thanks, and then we're off, an expedition rebooted.

The first few strokes of the paddle are within the calm water of the marina, but we soon leave its friendly confines to face the full brunt of the gale. This sudden shift from indoor couch potatoes back to paddling zealots is no gentle transition; it's as subtle as a shock delivered to bare skin by the cold, metal plates of a defibrillator. Within two minutes, my upper body is soaked, regularly bombarded by solid water breaking over the bow. I concentrate on maintaining a steady paddling rhythm and keeping my knees tucked up to prevent the waves from breaking open the Velcro fasteners of the spray skirt's front cockpit and flooding the canoe. Apart from these concerns and a grim sense of foreboding, my mind is blank.

It takes most of an hour to claw our way out of the bay, a distance of only three kilometres. We then turn north, rolling dangerously in the heavy, broadside swell. The only things that keep the two canoes upright are our headway and Chris and Jill's skillful steering. Although our perpendicular track is riskier than punching headfirst into the waves, it's drier for me, and my mind begins to function again. I hear a few bars from the Beach Boys' "Endless Summer" album playing in my head: "Catch a wave and you're sittin' on top of the world..." We're not quite at the top of the world, but we're catching our share of waves for sure. I've just learned that I have a subconscious

DJ with a sense of humour. I would never have consciously added that particular tune to today's mental playlist. But it's a good choice. I turn up the volume and let the tight vocal harmonies and innocent rhythms of 1960s California beach culture fill my mind with warmth and light.

After the required northward progress, we turn west into our inlet, ironically called "Sunshine Bay" by the Lupinites. The wind increases in velocity, and soon we're indeed riding the waves like surfers, corkscrewing and pitching as we go. These are the dreaded rear quartering winds, which I'm told are the worst conditions for keeping our Wenonahs on course. As usual, Jill seems to be managing okay. Chris and Christy are on a parallel course about 200 metres away, their twisting and sliding complementing our own gyrations in a complex syncopation that has all the makings of an informal, lacustrine dance party.

We continue for another 10 kilometres and then dip southward into a small channel leading to the head of our first portage towards Concession Lake, a 300-metre march across flat tundra. At the landing, the wind is so strong that I decide not to flip the canoe up to my shoulders. Instead, Jill and I carry it hull-side-down and low to the ground. It's difficult and awkward, but better than flying away like a leaf on a fall day. Chris manages to load his canoe on his shoulders in the conventional way and completes the portage while Christy holds the stern and keeps the boat aligned. Tired, suffering the shock of total re-immersion into a full-on wilderness setting, we pause at the end of the portage to wait out the idiosyncrasies of this strange tundra summer. Clothed in Gore-Tex and fleece, topped by my bright orange toque, I shiver for the first time on our trip. Malibu fades. Welcome to August in the north.

After a meal of pancakes, we pitch the bedroom tents and wriggle into their shelter, less spacious than Lupin's shopping mall environment, but entirely our own. As of 3:50 p.m. when I write this, strong winds continue, now accompanied by a hard, driving rain. We may be here for a while.

Camp Location: 65° 44.19'N 111° 26.42'W
Distance Today: 23 km. paddle, 0.3 km. portage
Distance to Date: 927 km. paddle, 27.9 km. portage

August 5

Yesterday's windbound camp became our overnight stop. When we wake up this morning, the tents are surrounded by overlapping puddles punctuated with short sprigs of soggy arctic willow. Had there been more rain, we might have awakened in the middle of a small lake. As it is, enough moisture has soaked through the tent bottoms to dampen the sleeping bags.

It takes discipline to pack our soggy bags and crawl stiffly out of the wet tents to face the dull, grey light of another cold, damp day. But soon, the many small chores we must complete before departure take over, crowding out dreary morning thoughts of damp bedding, aching shoulders and sore knees, and warming our bodies through activity. Our planned 7 a.m. departure is achieved, and we begin a rigorous, grinding regime of alternating paddle and portage as we continue towards Concession Lake.

Yesterday's east wind continues, driving the boats ahead of it and making the portages difficult. It's particularly challenging to land the canoes because the wind drives them towards rocky shorelines at a speed that's too fast for comfort. The only recourse is to back-paddle to slow the pace until the first scrape of rock on Kevlar is heard, and then it's all hands over the side and a wade to shore, hoping the water won't soak through the leather of our well-worn Bean Boots. Today's labour includes three portages of a total distance of 5 kilometres. As usual, we double-trip (forward, back and forward again), so our portaging amounts to 15 kilometres of scrambling over rock, muskeg and uneven ground; hard work, given that our packs are now bulging with the food collected at

Lupin.

I resort to a small history lesson to keep our perceived hardship in its proper perspective. Today, we cross paths with the route of Franklin's land expedition, which took place before his ill-fated quest for the Northwest Passage by sea. In September of 1821, Franklin and party were in slow, painful retreat from the Arctic Ocean, making for their base at Fort Providence, north of present-day Yellowknife. Although no lives had yet been lost, starvation had begun. By September 18th, they had gotten around the north end of Contwoyto and passed Concession Lake, near our present location. Franklin recorded: *"The next morning everyone was faint from hunger and marched with difficulty, having to oppose a fresh breeze and wade through snow 2 feet deep... The canoe was unfortunately broken by the fall of a person who had charge of it."* A month later, 10 were dead of starvation, exposure and in at least one case, murder. Sore muscles and damp gear do seem trivial by comparison.

We meet many caribou today, mostly in small groups, but sometimes as many as 20 at a time. They are at the same time timid and curious. Provided we make no sudden movement, they stand still and watch us; otherwise, they trot briskly away. Fat ptarmigans, seemingly less concerned, flutter about our feet as we portage.

During the day, the winds abate and the clouds part, revealing long-overdue sunshine, our first since Pellatt Lake six days ago. This evening it's calm, but clouds have returned. The temperature is 54°F. Who knows what meteorological variety tomorrow will bring?

We're camped at the southern end of an unnamed lake north of Concession, after a 12-hour working day. Located beside an esker, with a sandy beach, interesting hilly terrain in the background, and lots of caribou to observe, this is one of our better campsites since Great Slave. Two caribou entertain us by swimming the lake as we enjoy our supper of beef stroganoff. Their trails criss-cross the area and their bones are strewn on the beach, along with rusty tin cans, bits of cloth and other debris. Jill finds an ulu, a wooden-handled knife with a rusted semi-circular metal blade, used by Inuit to skin their kills. We photograph it, but Jill decides to leave it here. Who needs more weight to carry?

Speaking of debris, this evening's garbage burning is enlivened by the explosion of a small, metal canister that used to hold some of Chris's asthma medication. It's hidden in the waste that I toss onto my fire of dry twigs. Fortunately, the blaze was unattended when the thing exploded, scattering embers and small bits of shrapnel. For conspicuous gallantry in the face of danger, I win a promotion (in my own mind) from garbage control officer to mobile sanitation engineer.

Camp Location: 65° 43.98'N 111° 41.38'W
Distance Today: 9 km. paddle, 5.0 km. portage
Distance to Date: 936 km. paddle, 32.9 km. portage

Lupin Mine, where we fattened up for two wonderful days.

On the road again: Our first meal after Lupin Mine.

A sandy camp, north of Concession Lake.

The ulu.

Chapter 15: STOOD UP AT ROCKINGHORSE

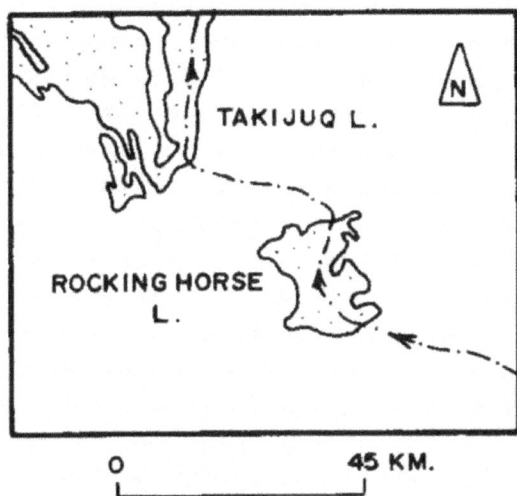

August 6

The day dawns cloudy, with a temperature of 40°F. We're up at 6 a.m. for a 7 a.m. departure. If it seems like the time between waking and paddling is short, it's because Chris's usual *modus operandi* requires us to earn our breakfast by putting in a few hours of travel beforehand. We get up, pack up and go, although we usually get to enjoy a half-litre hit of hot caffeine before pulling out.

There's still a strong east wind, but the lakes we're paddling are small, so we don't attach the spray skirts. It's a decision we regret. Near the north end of one lake, the wind increases until waves are breaking over the gunnels. I look over at Chris and Christy, expecting them to pull for the first available shelter. But no, their canoe turns eastward into the teeth of the gale and forges ahead. Jill turns our boat to follow.

"This is crazy," I mutter, as the water continues to splash into our boat from both sides. There's no chance to bail, and we're already getting bow-heavy. A few more minutes, and the water sluicing back and forth between the packs will tip us into the icy lake. It's too cold for swimming. But I shouldn't have worried; as usual, there's method in Chris' madness. After battering eastward for a scant half kilometre, we dodge north into a small narrows leading towards the next lake. Once in its shelter, we're freed from the wind's grasp and able to scoop the water from the canoes. During that brief dash to safety, I perfected my racing stroke, paddling with such vigour that my elbow was above my shoulder as I plunged the paddle down. On mornings like this, who needs coffee?

A few short portages follow, and we temporarily enter the watershed of the Coppermine River. During one of the portages, I find a rusted, "V"-shaped piece of metal protruding from the soft ground. Mystified, I give it a tug and out comes a formidable-looking leg-hold trap stamped "Oneida Community." Fortunately, it's not set. As with the traps we found back on Pike's Portage, Chris sets this one up and touches the pan with a stick. It responds with an energetic "clack!" satisfying an inner, boyish need on both our parts. We grin at each other. The women roll their eyes. The weight of our baggage is always on my mind, so I photograph this lethal piece of cultural history and leave it behind. Meanwhile, a band of 8 caribou walks by on a low rise, pausing briefly to stare at us.

After another short paddle, we take our boats and gear on a two-kilometre walk to Rockinghorse Lake. During the march, the sun comes out and the temperature soars, forcing us into shirt sleeves. The bugs, so little missed over the past few days, make a brief reappearance, their mobility hampered by the continuing wind. The cliffs of a small peninsula near the southeast corner of Rockinghorse Lake form a spectacular backdrop to the portage. We all pause to take photographs, setting our burdens down on the tops of large boulders conveniently scattered along our route. By the time the canoes, food and equipment are ferried across, the warmth has disappeared and the clouds have returned.

We set off up the east side of Rockinghorse at about

4:30 p.m., intending to get in another three hours of paddling, but by the time two hours have passed, it's plain that the wind and water are against us. Rather than cross a large bay broadside to the marching waves, we camp on a rocky island in the east-central part of the lake. Peregrine falcons nest here, and we see them soaring above us like kites in the slate-grey sky. As of 9:30 p.m., the wind continues. We plan another 7 a.m. start tomorrow.

This evening, I try a secret experiment. Due to various sins of omission and commission surrounding the care and management of a particular piece of luggage, some of our toilet paper has gotten wet. Trust me; few things are more frustrating than trying to unwind a soggy roll when in urgent need. Lumps of wet fluff pinched between thumb and forefinger won't do the job. But alternatives are available; on the snowy forest trails of northern Manitoba, we often made hygienic use of our empty lunch bags, buffing them between our knuckles until the brown paper became as soft and pliable as velour. Luxury! Now, the nearest brown paper is far away, and a different approach is needed. I decide to try an older solution: sphagnum moss. The first challenge is identifying it in the field. This is accomplished with the help of our "Naturalist's Guide," and I lay in a small supply, awaiting the call, which these days is regular and predictable. Once the duty is performed, I gingerly apply the moss: the cold, wet, earthy moss. Without going into a lot of technical detail, the sensation is unusual, but the results are satisfactory. I'm now psychologically prepared to function in a paperless society.

Camp Location: 65° 51.63'N 112° 12.82'W
Distance Today: 29 km. paddle, 2.6 km. portage
Distance to Date: 965 km. paddle, 35.5 km. portage

August 7

We're up at 6 a.m. and launch the boats an hour later.

It's overcast, but for the first time in several days, there's no wind to bother us. The wave-free water makes for easy paddling, but we keep the spray skirts fastened anyway, not trusting the day to keep its early promise.

Our immediate destination is the lake's northeast corner: out of our way, but potentially a worthwhile detour. Chris's Yellowknife contact at Gerle Gold mentioned another geological camp nearby and informed the camp manager that we might stop by. We arrive at the given coordinates, but there's nothing except a few rusted, 45-gallon drums and a dozing caribou. Disturbed by our arrival, the animal lurches to its feet, shakes its head from side to side and gazes stupidly at us for a few moments before staggering away, a vivid caricature of how some of us start our mornings these days.

We climb a small, conical hill and scan the surroundings, but there's no camp. Either our timing is wrong or our coordinates. There'll be no repetition of the good times we had back at Camp Vodka: no helicopter rides, hot showers or turkey dinner. We breakfast among the sandy hills and eskers that dominate this corner of the lake and then paddle northwest to where a river supposedly drains towards Takijuq Lake, sometimes called Napaktulik, about 25 kilometres away. No doubt, more portages await us as we continue our summer-long, subarctic biathlon.

At the north end of Rockinghorse, we're pleasantly surprised. After a short walk around a rock-studded rapid, we're able to drift down a narrow, fast-flowing watercourse. This is a canoeist's dream, drifting where we had expected to walk, floating easily past the few sandy shoals and scattered rocks. We paddle sporadically to keep the boats aligned with the flow. It reminds me of a log flume ride at an amusement park, but more sedate, and with much better scenery. Here, we run our first whitewater. It's a set of ripples about as long as the canoes and maybe twice as wide; nonetheless, Jill and I twirl our paddles and hoot according to the time-honoured custom. Chris regards us thoughtfully from the other canoe, as if he knows something we don't.

The river widens, and we enter a chain of small lakes. Chris's fishing rod, which disappointed us during the last few days, delivers two medium-sized trout, assuring us of a fish dinner. The sun shines, the temperature climbs, and the bugs swarm in quick succession.

While paddling these rock-bound lakes and inhaling flying insects, I'm able to confirm a long-held suspicion by direct observation. I hereby attest that mosquitoes, at least in this part of the country, park themselves on deep, open lake water, supported by surface tension, and take off to attack us as we pass. They do not, as I had thought, sniff us out from the nearest bog and fly across the water to seek their meal. I don't suppose they wait on the lake to ambush rare, passing canoeists. They're probably blown offshore and settle on the water's surface to rest. No doubt, a few become food for the fish we enjoy so much. With this knowledge, tonight's trout will taste even better. What better revenge on the blood-sucking bugs than to skip up the food chain a few levels and eat them? We might even recover some of our own stolen protein. It's great to be an omnivore!

About one-third of the way between Rockinghorse and Takijuq, we have a decision to make: either land and make a one-and-a-half-kilometre portage across a height of land, or paddle to the lakes' outlet and try our luck again on the river. Chris' recent maps, prepared from satellite imagery, show a thin, blue line suggesting a dubious passage at best. My older set, prepared at the same scale but based on aerial photographs, shows a wider, more obvious passage with a defined set of rapids. We decide to follow the river. It turns out that the reality is better than either chart. Here once again is our winding, sandy river. Floating through the rapid shown on my map, we see only a placid stream.

We end our paddling day on this happy note, pulling over to the riverbank to raise the cook tent, completing the job just as a heavy rain begins. Next, we begin the important task of cooking and eating all the fresh lake trout we can handle. Chris fries the deboned fillets in butter, adding just the right amount of lemon pepper seasoning. We enjoy our dinner in the tepee as the rain pelts down outside.

As of 9 p.m., the rain has stopped, but the sky remains overcast. Outside, the bugs are swarming, lusting for payback, but we're snug in our tents, stomachs full, lounging, reading, writing and dreaming. This is life as it should be lived. Scribbling these notes in these warm, safe surroundings, I have no wish to be anywhere else. Tomorrow, all being well, we'll reach Takijuq Lake and begin our journey's last big-water traverse: 55 kilometres due north to the Arctic Circle and the headwaters of the Hood River. Once there, we'll start a long, downhill run to the Polar Sea at Arctic Sound, an exciting journey in its own right.

Camp Location: 66° 02.08'N 112° 29.84'N
Distance Today: 36 km. paddle, 0.5 km. portage
Distance to Date: 1001 km. paddle, 36 km. portage

Chapter 16: HUBRIS AND NEMESIS

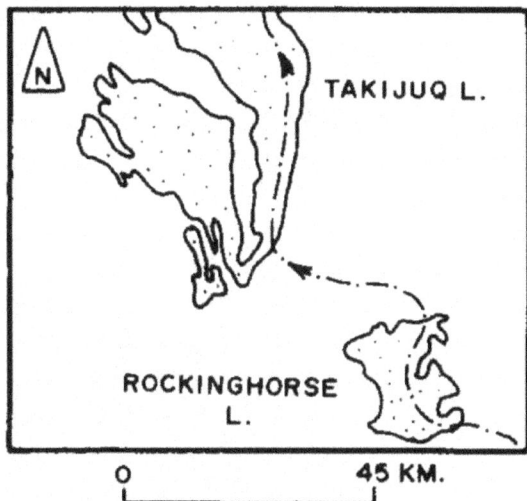

August 8

While northbound out of Rockinghorse
On a narrow, foam-flecked watercourse,
We struck a rock with deadly force,
And fractured the canoe, of course.

Yesterday's hubris has been rewarded. While running a modest Class 2 rapid, Jill and I have a head-on collision with a submerged boulder. Before we can react, the canoe rides up this rocky shelf and pivots broadside to the current, leaving Jill and me dangling out in the flow at either end. There's an ominous cracking sound as the boat heels over to a 45-degree angle. I twist around, expecting to see Jill and the back half of the canoe twirling away in the torrent. But it holds together, a testament to the skill of its makers and our dumb luck. We climb out onto the slippery rock and balance there, manhandling the boat until it's pointing downstream. We then slide back into our seats and push ourselves free, completing the rapid and then paddling over to an eddy on the right side of the river to collect ourselves.

While teetering out on that rock, I thought that our trip was over, and that in a few short seconds we'd be swimming. We avoid that, but there's still a price to pay. The canoe's aluminum thwart is broken clean in two, and the resin coating along the keel is badly cracked near the middle of the boat. Also, a Kevlar patch Chris had installed last year after another mishap has pulled away from the hull.

Examining the damage, Chris whistles and says in his best Christopher Robin voice, "Gee, that's too bad! I feel so sad for you." He suggests we name the canoe "See-Saw" because of its recent balancing act, and asks us if we could please do it again for his camera. Chris's teasing banter is annoying, but his foresight in fabricating and pre-drilling a second thwart back at Camp Vodka saves the trip for Jill and me. Within two hours, he has replaced the broken thwart with our homemade one and fastened it to the gunnels using the rivet gun flown in to us at Vodka. Skillful application of Kevlar and resin from the repair kit will soon restore the hull to a condition that will theoretically allow it to finish the trip. With its weakened keel, it will be of little value to Chris for future wilderness excursions. This means that Jill and I have "bought the boat" and owe him a sum to be determined later. Our vehicle should still be suitable for a lifetime of sedate, flat-water paddling. Jill and I have yet to work out the details of ownership; will I buy her half, or will she buy mine? Since I live in Toronto and she in Ottawa, joint custody isn't practical. But we'll only have to settle the issue if our fractured Wenonah survives the rest of the journey. If not, Chris suggests that we douse it with naphtha, strike a match, and send the flaming wreckage over a waterfall. "Think of the great pictures!" he chortles gleefully. Obviously, he has no sentimental bonds with his equipment, and it's probably just as well.

The incident puts a damper on our early morning, but our tourists' instincts are still intact. Shutters click as Jill and I stand sheepishly beside the inverted, cracked canoe, our paddles resting blade-first on the ground like the rifle butts of African big-game hunters posing beside a kill. All this happens before breakfast. We eat our pancakes at the crash site and then resume our journey. A short distance downriver, we come upon an abandoned geological camp including six wood-framed, canvas-sided tents, the inevitable stockpile of fuel drums and a corrugated metal shed, full of carefully catalogued drill cores. We land, and Chris scavenges a few nuts, bolts and washers from the derelict tents, "In case those rivets pop out." We spend another 45 minutes or so poking around our find, and trying to decipher the curious graffiti left by a bored, departed occupant. It's either a frank, metaphorical commentary on the loneliness of camp life, or a desperate cry for psychological help.

The sun comes out, the temperature climbs, the bugs swarm and Chris catches two trout. In the immortal words of Yogi Berra, it's déjà vu all over again. Even the scenery is the same as yesterday's. If we're trapped in a time loop, I hope we avoid the rock this time.

The final portage to Takijuq Lake is a spectacular, kilometre-long hike along the rim of a narrow canyon that compresses our river into a foaming torrent. Clear skies offer a pleasing backdrop for photos of the rocky crags, the distant lake, the gorge, etc.

While hauling our second loads into our campsite on Takijuq's gravel beach, we hear an aircraft high overhead. Chris examines it through the zoom lens of his camera and declares, "It's an Air Tindi Twin Otter!" He pulls out his VHF radio from the ever-present grey, waterproof case, thumbs the transmit button and makes a call. This time, he's more business-like than during the abortive doughnut transaction.

"Twin Otter over Takijuq Lake. Twin Otter over Takijuq Lake. Come in, please."

"This is the Twin Otter. Go ahead."

"This is the Chris Morris canoe party. Are you Air Tindi?"

"Affirmative."

"You guys are scheduled to pick us up at Arctic Sound on August 28, 29 or 30. Please tell your office we are on schedule and everything here is okay."

"Affirmative. You are on schedule and everything is okay."

"That's right. Thanks. Out."

With that, we've made direct contact with the outside world for the first time since Lupin. If we disappear, they'll know where to start looking. The need for rescue seems unlikely, but today's events are food for thought. If Jill and I had managed to do a proper job of scuttling our canoe, Chris and Christy would have completed the trip alone (one hopes), met our chartered plane at the coast, and ridden it back to the scene of the crime to pick up Jill and me, along with some souvenir fragments of aluminum and Kevlar. In the meantime, we'd have had the pleasure of sitting and ruminating in a tent for at least three weeks, awaiting an uncertain retrieval and making plaintive journal entries.

Despite the potential alternatives, we're all sitting together at the southeast corner of Takijuq Lake, gazing at the rolling hills of its long, central peninsula while listening to the muted roar of whitewater from the canyon to our rear. I won't commit hubris for the second time in as many days, but life could certainly be worse. I top the evening off with an enthusiastic garbage incineration. Tomorrow it's northward on Takijuq, weather permitting.

Camp Location: 66° 04.52'N 112° 50.26'W
Distance Today: 14 km. paddle, 2.5 km. portage
Distance to Date: 1015 km. paddle, 38.5 km. portage

A caribou eyes us with justifiable suspicion (Chris Morris).

Big-game hunters with their kill (Chris Morris).

View from the final portage to Takijuq Lake.

Treading carefully on Takijuq Lake (Chris Morris).

Chapter 17: ACROSS THE ARCTIC CIRCLE

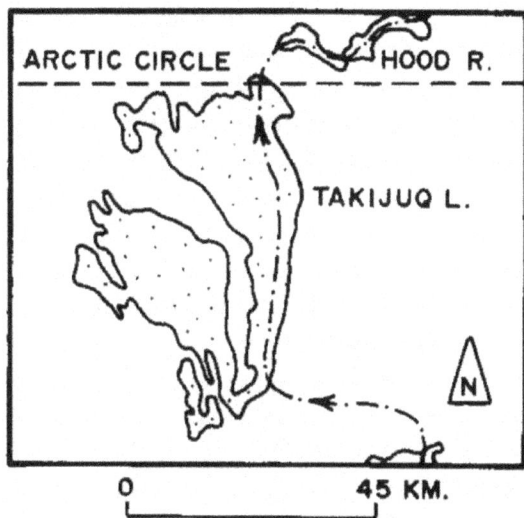

August 9

   We're up at 7 a.m. for an 8 a.m. departure. Takijuq, calm last night, has grown restless, goaded by a northwest wind. Loading the canoes in the surf is a challenge: lots of wading and balancing and bracing of knees against lively gunnels.

   The weather is cooperative for most of today's paddle, the early morning's windy chop dwindling to a dead calm. Later, several clusters of rain clouds float across the northern horizon from west to east. The streamers of precipitation resemble slender, silvery legs, and in my mind, the clouds become giant, sky-borne spiders, stalking the tundra in search of prey. We avoid most of them, but we're caught near the lake's north end, enduring a cold, intense 15-minute deluge while winds whip the lake into whitecaps. This is nothing new, except that Jill and I are keenly aware of each bump and roll of our boat's crippled keel. We'll be glad once the follow-up repairs are completed in the headwaters of the Hood.

Our prolonged traverse of Takijuq requires a couple of one-hour breaks on the shore to refuel, plus several other brief pauses while remaining on the water. During one of the latter, our leader is forced by circumstances to tinkle into his coffee mug (P ubi non curamus).

"Hey Chris," I call, while observing the proceedings. "That's one thing I have that's bigger than yours!" As he glances down involuntarily, I quickly clarify, "No, I mean my bladder!" I was able to do my business exclusively on land today.

We reach Takijuq's north shore at around 7:30 p.m. I check the GPS and confirm that we've reached the Arctic Circle, that parallel of latitude above which there's at least one day without sunrise (in winter) and without sunset (in summer). Thousands cross this circumpolar boundary every day in the comfort of high-flying commercial jets, and in some places people drive across it in buses, cars and bicycles. Still, it's especially satisfying to have reached this latitude by walking and paddling across the trackless tundra. There's a small ceremony, which consists mainly of attaching cameras to Chris's tripod, setting the timers and getting group shots of us standing around, scratching and grinning. We're too tired and bug-infested to do much else.

We conclude the day with a 500-metre portage to our current camp. The walk is more strenuous for me than usual because the damaged canoe has taken water into its forward floatation tank. At first, I think I'm having a major physical malfunction, but as the bow continues to thud into the ground in front of me, I figure it out. More canoe damage isn't good news, but I'm relieved the fault doesn't lie with my arms and shoulders. I'm going to need them for a while longer. Other body parts aren't doing so well; my mind is so foggy that instead of emptying the water from the bow, I add more weight to the stern of the boat to compensate. Muscle or brain, I suppose we each work with whatever tools are most readily available. As my own physical capacity increases, I'm working harder, not smarter: circumstantial evidence that brain size really is inversely proportional to muscle mass.

Tomorrow, we plan to log just a few kilometres, and then spend the rest of the day resting and repairing equipment in preparation for our source-to-mouth passage of the Hood River. In particular, we hope to make good the remaining damage to the See-Saw. The pause will give the cold-cure resin time to set.

Camp Location: 66° 33.50'N 112° 55.50'W
Distance Today: 54 km. paddle, 0.5 km. portage
Distance to Date: 1069 km. paddle, 39 km. portage

Chapter 18: THEY GAVE THEIR ALL

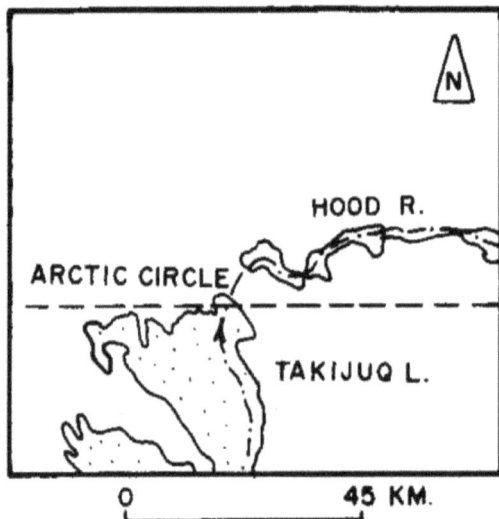

August 10

We start the day with a brief paddle, followed by a portage across the low divide between the watershed of the Coppermine River and the headwaters of the Hood. We reach our present camp at noon. It's all downhill from here to our rendezvous with Air Tindi at Arctic Sound.

After a late breakfast, we pitch the cook tent astride the See-Saw and Chris begins the required surgery, applying pre-cut Kevlar patches soaked in cold-cure resin. The worst damage was sustained in the middle of the boat, where a vertical, spring-loaded "pogo stick" connects the centre thwart to the keel. Three overlapping patches are applied, and the base of the pogo stick is reattached, using bolts set into the cold-cure. I don't know what we could have done by way of repairs if we hadn't carried the required materials with us. Even if the reconstruction is successful, we'll have to stay put until the resin cures, at least overnight and maybe into the next day. Our earlier hard work means we're ahead of schedule and can afford the time. Here's a good rule of thumb for marathon, wilderness canoeing: always go while the going is good, so you don't have to go when it's not (or something like that).

Today's temperature is about 58°F with gusty winds from the west, grey skies and scattered showers. A thunder squall greeted the end of our portage, causing us to scramble to get the loose gear undercover before the rain fell. It's incredible how fast a person can move when highly motivated, even when carrying a heavy pack over fields of boulders. Dryness is warmth and security; dampness means cold discomfort. That's why I hesitate to do a much-needed laundry. Today, I'd rather wear dry, dirty clothes than clean, clammy ones.

As I sit in the tent writing this entry, Jill and Chris are off for a walk, and Christy is napping in another tent. A few moments ago, my writing was interrupted by a muffled thump when the kitchen tent blew over. After a few minutes spent wrestling with the billowing fabric, order was restored. The primary concern was to keep the material from gluing itself to the sticky resin on the fractured canoe.

Later, a Twin Otter flies directly over the camp at low altitude from south to north. After about an hour, it returns on a reciprocal bearing. Based on its bright yellow colour, we speculate that it's a military search and rescue aircraft based in Yellowknife. We hope they found whoever it was they were looking for. These intermittent encounters with aircraft are noteworthy because they assure us that life goes on, out in the wider world.

We didn't plan it, but this crash-induced layover is a welcome opportunity to rest tired bodies and reflect on our journey so far. This evening, after supper, in a nostalgic and contemplative mood, we pay tribute to the equipment that has made the ultimate sacrifice to enable our little expedition to proceed. Here's an honour roll of things lost or broken:

One camera lens cap (drowned in Toura Lake)
Two aluminum canoe thwarts (broken)

One hat with a wide brim and ear flaps, named "Fuddette"
(blown out of a canoe on Great Slave Lake)
One Casio electronic wristwatch (now beeping a perpetual
reveille every morning at 6 a.m., near the edge of Glowworm
Lake)
One electronic wind gauge (accidentally dropped into a dense
thicket of shrubs south of Pellatt Lake and reluctantly
abandoned after an intensive search)
One fuel cap for a Coleman stove (stolen by a raven)
One Swiss army knife (gone AWOL)
One plastic spoon (disappeared)
One plastic dish (ran away with the spoon, probably)
One plastic knife (possibly still involved with the dish)
One tent fly (decommissioned and incinerated near Artillery
Lake)
One fishing rod tip (sunk in Great Slave Lake)
Two fishing lures (lost while on duty)
One sinker for a fishing line (sunk)
One Coleman stove (retired as unserviceable)
One stainless steel Gerber knife (broken while vigorously
assisting in a canoe repair)
One casting reel (discharged, dead)
Several metal tent pegs (embedded in some lonely, distant
patch of tundra that is forever England)

*Editor's Note: The author also lost about 10 pounds from his
already lean frame, but did not discover this until later.*

    I don't think the above is evidence that we've been
unduly careless. On a trip of this magnitude, the various minor
incidents, accidents and omissions are magnified simply by
duration. Foresight, luck, and occasional bursts of ingenuity
mean that nothing vital has been lost or damaged beyond
repair.
    On a happier note, we would be remiss in not
welcoming some goods and equipment acquired along our
route by various means:

One Maglite "Mini-Mag" flashlight (found on an island in
Great Slave Lake)
One metal fork (accidentally acquired from our friends at
Pike's Portage)
One rivet gun and related supplies (flown in to Camp Vodka)
Several litres of naphtha (obtained at Lupin Mine)
Many pounds of fresh lake trout (yanked abruptly from
various lakes and rivers)
Other food (acquired or consumed at Hoarfrost River, Pike's
Portage, Camp Vodka and Lupin Mine)

Later, I consider our group's ability not only to tolerate
but to enjoy such an extended camping trip. I believe that some
wouldn't have prospered as we have, and I wonder where our
advantages lie. One trick we've employed is to adapt rather
than endure. During a weekend trip, it's easy to withstand or
even embrace discomfort. Temporary hunger, cold and fatigue
come with bragging rights and increase the enjoyment of the
oncoming hamburger, hot shower or warm bed. On our
current journey, that kind of endurance isn't a sane option, and
even though we sometimes suffer in a small way, we don't
consider it a virtue. Our equipment reflects this philosophy.
Our clothing (poly-pro, fleece and Gore-Tex) provides all the
required protection against wind and weather. Food and
baggage are packed in durable, rubberized dry bags,
waterproof (when properly packed and closed), and equipped
with waist belts to spare our shoulders the full weight of their
contents. Our tents don't leak. The canoes are light and fast,
and a joy to paddle. We spent a lot of money on equipment,
but none of us has regretted our purchases (except for a
recently acquired half of a fractured canoe).

It's also important that each of us is identically
equipped with boots, mugs and other paraphernalia. Had we
not taken this precaution, the perceived injustice of (for
example) one person having access to tall, waterproof boots,
while another had to make do with canvas runners, would

probably have been a source of dissension in the ranks and a licence to complain.

And then there are those pesky, people factors that seldom appear on gear checklists. Bugs will bite and caribou will flee, but who knows what a person will do? And what they do today doesn't predict what they'll do tomorrow. One thing's for sure: group morale always suffers when two or more alpha personalities duke it out for control. Our advantage is the willingness of 75% of the group to compromise and accommodate. Just call us the silent majority. Chris, the remaining 25% is outspoken, opinionated and firmly in charge. The rest of us bite our tongues and suck it up, knowing that, whatever his faults, Chris works hard and knows what he's doing. All in all, his is a benevolent dictatorship, governing with the consent of the people, and focused on making sure we achieve our summer's goal. Without him, the trip would never have gotten this far. He knows it, and so do we. We therefore grant him the stage and podium, content for the most part to sit in the audience and clap politely. With just one ego to feed, we're generally happy campers. Despite the emotional highs and lows, the mood in the tents and in the canoes has remained cheery out of all proportion to the circumstances. Even when we're inconvenienced, we remain enthusiastic about our summer's task, well aware that we have the privilege of enjoying something that others can only dream about. That said, we've not yet been able to match the "joie de vie" of Anderson and Stewart's 1855 expedition, which allowed Anderson to report, *"Immediately after breakfast the portage was begun and...at about 10:30 p.m. our fine fellows were descending a steep mountain with the canoes singing La Violette."*

Time for bed. The resin is still hardening and will take another 18 hours to cure at current temperatures. We won't be pulling out early tomorrow. In fact, we may spend the entire day at our current location. If so, I hope the temporary stability will inspire me to wash my smelly long-johns.

Camp Location: 66° 34.94'N 112° 53.24'N
Distance Today: 3.0 km. paddle, 1.5 km. portage
Distance to Date: 1072 km. paddle, 40.5 km. portage

August 11

Thanks to yesterday's canoe surgery, we're up at the lazy hour of 9 a.m., one of our latest sleep-ins to date. My bladder was stretched to the size of a basketball, but I managed to stay snugly wrapped in my Woods Caribou mummy bag, which I've finally learned to operate at its maximum thermal efficiency. (Don't try to roll around inside a mummy bag; just wear it like clothing.)

Outside it's cold and windy with light rain, so we sit in the cook tent, talking, reading and writing. The remaining Coleman stove is gently purring under the inverted canoe to speed the curing of the resin. True to yesterday's resolution, I did my laundry earlier, using Gore-Tex mitts as protection from the cold water. The lucky clothing is now draped over the hull of the canoe, steaming in the warmth from the stove beneath.

To help pass the time, I ask Chris and Christy to explain in general terms the subjects of their upcoming doctoral studies. My dull mind struggles to absorb the resulting flow of information. I ask Chris if he can please explain his topic in a short, simple paragraph. "No, I can't," he says, but tries anyway. Apparently, he'll attempt to address the question of morality versus rationality using some obscure form of mathematics. Christy's area of interest is some aspect of bioethics. Again, I can't grasp the details. I seek other distractions, but the only book currently available is a biography of Albert Einstein, complete with a lengthy description of his famous theory. This was Christy's contribution to the expedition's library. Whatever happened to light entertainment? Jill reads "A Naturalist's Guide to the Arctic." I watch the steam curling up from my drying underwear.

Camp Location: 66° 34.94'N 112° 53.24'W
Distance Today: 0 km. paddle, 0 km. portage
Distance to Date: 1072 km. paddle, 40.5 km. portage

Chris strikes a pose as we near the Arctic Circle.

Canoe hospital in the headwaters of the Hood River.

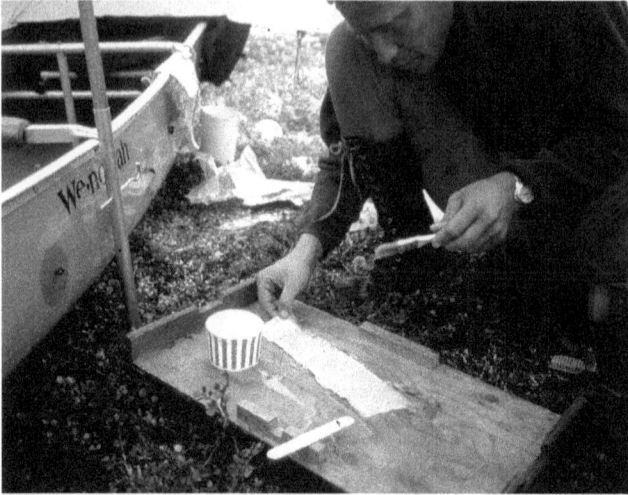

The surgeon at work: applying resin to a piece of Kevlar cloth.

One of many Hood River rapids.

Chapter 19: A BROAD, BRAWNY BACK

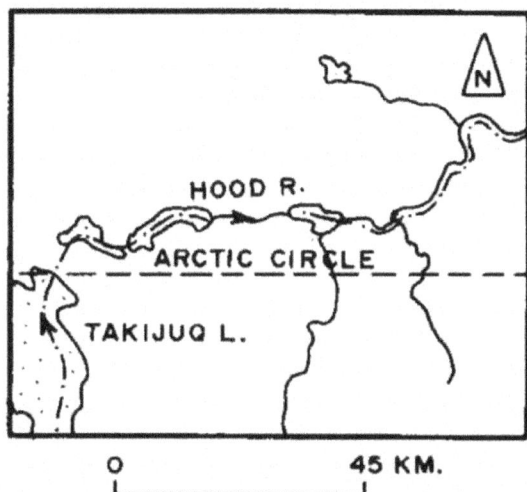

August 12

This is my paddle.
There are many others like it, but this one is mine.
My paddle is my best friend. It is my life.
I must master it as I must master my life.
Without me, my paddle is useless.
Without my paddle, I am useless...

Up at 6 a.m. and paddling at 7, making an eastward passage through the chain of lakes that form the headwaters of the Hood. It's tiring, mainly because of a cold and constant headwind. There's also a residual sluggishness due to our day off yesterday. It feels like a Monday.

The rapids in this reach of the river (we portage three of them today) are rock-choked and offer little opportunity for running or lining. Chris and Christy have a problem with a small riffle, running aground, and having to get out and push. No damage to the canoe and no danger, but the first paddling difficulty the maestro has exhibited this trip. Jill and I choose to portage. It's only a 20-metre carry-over and we don't want to expose our battered craft to any unnecessary abuse. Call it pride of ownership. Other than the hard work, today's time on the river is unremarkable, and we quit after making 35 kilometres.

Tonight's camp is located near the foot of a scenic waterfall at the bottom end of a brief portage. Shortly after we arrive, Chris casts his line into the pool at the base of the falls to see what the river will yield. Within five minutes, he has landed three medium-sized trout. I surprise myself with the vigour and enthusiasm with which I beat their brains out with a rock to keep them from flopping back into the water. Someone less hungry would probably have more sympathy for the fish. These three, along with two others caught while trolling the headwater lakes, allow us to enjoy another all-you-can-eat buffet, with the usual accompaniment of instant mashed potatoes, salt, pepper and butter. I don't think I could ever tire of such a meal, especially the all-you-can-eat feature. Chris had planned on catching enough fish over the length of the trip for about 16 meals. With today's haul, we only need enough fish for two more dinners, but as long as Chris is willing to keep catching, we'll be willing to keep eating. Incidentally, those who would consider living from rod to mouth might be interested in a statistic cited by Malcolm Waldron in his 1931 character study of John Hornby, "Snow Man." Waldron reported that to maintain body weight, a hard-working paddler on the barrens living on an all-fish diet requires 12 pounds of fish per day. For the budget-minded adventurer, that works out to a daily ration of about 27 cans of tuna.

The bugs are manageable this evening, and there's no rain, so we forgo the cook tent. As we lounge comfortably on the open tundra, digesting our fish feed, Chris and I begin a heated phase of our ongoing debate about liberalism in Western society and where it might lead. At first, I think I'm gaining the upper hand. Not so. Never argue with a philosopher; when cornered, they always manage to shift their ground, restating their initial premise in a subtle way that side-steps a carefully crafted argument. Soon, I'm the one cornered.

Our verbal jousting is interrupted by the thumping of a helicopter following our route along the line of the river. The sound swells as the chopper bursts over the horizon at the top of the falls, making further conversation impossible. We're surprised when the pilot pulls his machine into a banking, low-altitude turn and orbits our camp, observing us closely from his tilting, Plexiglass cockpit. Sprawled on the tundra like Roman senators at a banquet, not sure of the proper etiquette for welcoming uninvited aircraft, we wave politely. The pilot waves back. Apparently satisfied, he reverses direction and returns upstream. The thumping fades until the sound of flowing water is again audible. After scratching our heads, we decide that there's an office pool going on back at Lupin Mine about our rate of progress. They must have sent out the helicopter to settle the bets. Our guess is probably wrong, but the flypast makes us feel important, the focus of a distant someone's concern. If you really want to reach out and touch someone on the barrens, a helicopter is definitely the way to go.

We turn in for the night, anticipating another early departure tomorrow. During the night, the wind builds and the noise of it beating against the fabric walls of the tents competes with the sound of the waterfall. The thermometer would have us believe that it's 50°F outside, but it feels much colder.

Camp Location: 66° 38.54'N 112° 12.12'W
Distance Today: 35 km. paddle, 0.7 km. portage
Distance to Date: 1107 km. paddle, 41.2 km. portage

August 13

After a night of gales so strong I feared for the tents, the day dawns to a diminished but constant wind from the northeast. The sky to the west is a menacing, dark grey, while to the east it's clear. This half-and-half sky persists for much of the morning as some sort of frontal system slides sideways across our path. In the late afternoon, there's sunshine, and the wind continues to drop.

Most of today's work consists of portages, five in all. They're short but tiring, coming in quick succession, with just a few intervening strokes of the paddle. So far, we haven't had much benefit from traveling in a downstream direction. Most of the current is concentrated in the short, rock-studded drops between the lakes. Some of the rapids we portage today are runnable, but this river is too remote to take unnecessary chances. Now that we know our canoes aren't immortal, none of us wants to risk a wrecked boat and a premature end to our voyage, now nearing its grand finale at the Arctic Ocean. We won't be able to avoid every rapid, but it's best to be selective.

By 2 p.m., we're out of gas and stop for a hot lunch of minestrone and cheese, supplemented as usual by raisins, peanuts and chocolate. The pit stop gives us the energy to climb back into our Kevlar envelopes and finish an 11½-hour day, gliding into our current location near the downstream end of a seven-kilometre-long lake, at about 6:30 p.m.

This evening, I score a rare, verbal, knockout victory over our expedition's leader and philosopher-in-chief. It's after dinner and he's delivering a lengthy diatribe on the fallacy of absolute morality: no right or wrong, it's all relative...something along that vein. I don't think Chris believes most of what he's saying, but he likes to try these arguments on for size, confident that his followers don't have the verbal muscle to challenge him, let alone bring him down. Now in full flight, he continues to build his argument: those who judge others are always wrong...no absolute standards of behaviour...blah, blah, blah. Sometimes, he's a real windbag. Hmmm. Wind. Suddenly, I have an idea. If Chris is true to form, it just might work. And we did have beans for supper. I decide to go for it. As he continues his incontinent monologue, I look him squarely in the eye and interrupt the flow of words with a resounding, hearty belch, followed closely by a loud noise from the other end. As I'd hoped, my top-to-bottom rebuttal causes Chris to wrinkle his nose in disgust.

"You are <u>so</u> foul!"

I spring my trap. "By what standard do you judge me foul?"

Chris opens his mouth and then closes it again. Incredibly, he's been put to silence. Muhammad Ali has hit the mat face-first! I savour the moment, knowing it's not likely to be repeated.

Camp Location: 66° 38.92'N 111° 45.82'W
Distance Today: 17 km. paddle, 1.8 km. portage
Distance to Date: 1124 km. paddle, 43.0 km. portage

August 14

*"Looks like whitewater ahead," said the canoeist, **rapidly**.*

We're up at 7 a.m. and on the river an hour later. Today's action includes one short portage and three brief rapids. Jill and I are least successful on the first, catching a rock and breaking off a piece of the canoe's skid plate, a protective pad of Kevlar glued to the front of the keel. There's no other damage, and the resultant small crater is filled in using five-minute epoxy. We do better on the next, running it as well as could be expected, given its shallow, rock-studded configuration and the large turning radius of our flat-keeled canoes. Yes, I know that a poor worker blames his tools, but I also know that both boats are going to take a real beating in the days ahead.

The last rapid is the most culturally significant of the three. Hoping to learn something valuable from the fate of the other canoe, Jill and I perch on a rock at the edge of the river and watch intently as Chris and Christy begin their run. Aware of our intense gaze, and revelling in the attention, Chris suddenly stands up in the stern of his canoe, still grasping his paddle and attempts to expose his own stern. Unfortunately (for him, not us), he can't get his pants down with his one free hand. The canoe sideswipes a rock, forcing him to sit abruptly on his still-hidden posterior and return his attention to the water. He and Christy finish their run without further complications.

Inspired by this attempted display of youthful bravado, Jill and I work out a plan whereby we'll beat the rapid by cutting left, then right, avoiding this rock, skirting that hole, etc., ending up on a smooth tongue of boulder-clear water. Returning quickly to the canoe, we try to execute our scheme while it's still fresh in our minds. Unfortunately, once in the rapid, things happen too fast, and the glare of the sun in our eyes is too strong, so our plan unravels in short order. Then it's a case of "chacun sauve qu'il peut," taking it one rock at a time and hoping for the best. And the best is what we get. The canoe squeezes between two large boulders with only a gentle, grating protest and then shoots over the final drop like a torpedo, splashing energetically into the deeper water below. As we complete our run, we notice that Chris has his camera out. He was sure we would end up swimming and was ready to record the event. He seems offended by our success. It's an attitude typical of the cold-blooded media. One person's misfortune is another's news event. I think, "Damn all reporters!"

Today, for the first time, we pass through a few narrow reaches where there's discernible current without rapids. Thanks to this, and a tailwind, we're able to truly motor through these narrows. Maybe it's a preview of what awaits downstream. My image of us riding the broad, brawny back of the mighty Hood River to the shores of the Polar Sea may yet become a reality. Jill and I both hope that our battered Wenonah holds together for two more weeks and is able to retire from arctic service with dignity, after its second consecutive summer on the barrens.

This evening, I light another fire. I mention this only because when I throw a smouldering stick into the water to extinguish it, the charred wood is set upon by a large trout that makes repeated and unsuccessful attempts to pull it below the surface. I excitedly point this out to Chris and try to persuade him to drop in a line, but he declines, no doubt worn out by his recent whitewater exploits.

Camp Location: 66° 47.31'N 111° 11.84'W
Distance Today: 36 km. paddle, 0.5 km. portage
Distance to Date: 1160 km. paddle, 43.5 km. portage

Chapter 20: FOOTPRINTS IN THE SAND

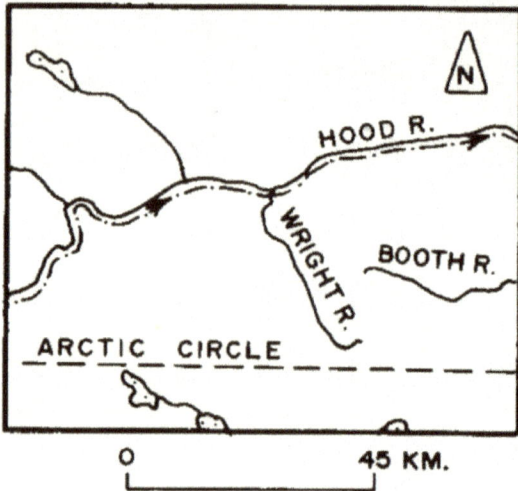

August 15

This morning it's warm, calm and sunny for a change. We're up at 6 a.m. and away at 7, our departure hastened by swarms of black flies, also up early to enjoy the pleasant weather.

Since portaging across the Arctic Circle on the 9th of August, we've been travelling through a rugged, granitic plateau, studded with rocky, knob-like hills. After the first hour and a half of today's paddling, we leave the headwater lakes and plateau behind at a point where the Hood narrows within a valley of sandy hills, well-pitted with animal tracks. We immediately feel the strong pull of the river. After all the weeks of neutral current, it's strange but pleasant to be carried along in the flow. There are no more lakes to paddle; there's only this river left to run.

Two kilometres beyond this transition, we're forced to pull out, just upstream of a nasty Class 5 rapid, surging through a narrow gorge carved through a bedrock outcrop. It's a picturesque setting, with billowing whitewater and rocky terrain in the foreground, framed by a line of sandy hills. Back from the gorge, there's a well-worn portage trail, another novelty. We walk its 500-metre length, taking frequent detours to the chasm to view the rushing water.

Three kilometres further on, we run a short but rocky Class 2 rapid. Chris and Christy pass through cleanly; Jill and I impart a gentle kiss to a rock with the stern of our canoe, another scratch engraved on the bottom of the hull, another summer souvenir. Next up is a kilometre-long, Class 3 challenge, studded with rocks. Jill and I decide not to run it. Chris says our decision shows a "pissy attitude," since we hadn't viewed the entire stretch before making up our minds. In fact, we saw enough to judge its difficulty against our skill level and made the decision with a clear conscience. Chris and Christy join us in our portage, and nothing more is said. Two small chutes below the portage are run without difficulty. Downstream of the chutes is a series of swifts and shoals where the river exhibits braiding and forms a wider, sand-filled channel.

Our next stop is about eight kilometres downstream, another spectacular Class 5 rapid. From our vantage point on the left side of the channel, we can see the rapid's entire 1 kilometre length and the broad, sandy river valley in the distance below. This gorge and the last are formed by ribs of exposed bedrock running perpendicular to the river. There's no debate about how to handle this boat-eater, and we complete a portage, doing the dog and pony show with the canoes because of a moderate westerly wind.

A short distance further downstream, there are two successive chutes with relatively few rocks to avoid, each followed by clearly discernible tongues of smooth water. Large standing waves at the end promise a moderate thrill. The first chute is run cleanly by both canoes. After watching Chris and Christy make a clean run of the second, Jill and I make our attempt. We keep to the right of a deep, boiling hole and then try to claw our way to smooth water on the far left. As usual, we find a rock and deal it a glancing blow with our careworn watercraft. I don't know what conversations the others have as they skip through the rocks, but here's a typical example of the teamwork in our boat:

Me: "Rock ahead."

Jill: "What?"

Me: "There's a rock ahead!"

Jill: "Left, or right?"

Me: "What?"

Jill: "Should we go left, or right?"

Me: "I think...maybe...." Crash!

I don't blame Jill. As a bow paddler, it's my job to avoid such hazards, and so far, I've been less than proficient. But I do think that installing an intercom in the boat would help.

During today's paddle, we pass under the flight path used by aircraft servicing a major mining development called Ulu, a gold mine in the making, north of the Hood. When this mine goes into production in a couple of years, the winter road from Yellowknife will be extended, and the ore will be hauled by truck back to Lupin for processing. During the dark, frigid winter months, it will therefore be possible to drive a car to a point above the Hood River. I'd like to try it, but not in my ancient Dodge.

A kilometre or two later, we're at the upstream end of a 30-foot-high waterfall. There are many footprints on the beach, and "August 12 noon" is inscribed in the sand. So, we know there's one other party on the Hood, three days ahead of us: crowded conditions for the subarctic. We camp on the south side of the river at the downstream end of the falls.

Shortly after our arrival, the sky clouds up and deals us a cold, driving rain. We pitch the cook tent and eat our pasta meal indoors. Later in the evening, Chris catches our first grayling of the trip, along with two small lake trout. One of the latter mysteriously vanishes, and a fat gull perched on a nearby sandbar is a prime suspect. Also inhabiting the vicinity of our camp are a few tame, well-fed ground squirrels. This is bad news for our food packs, so we're careful to keep things sealed up.

After supper, I sit beside the rapids below the falls. Enveloped in mist, I stare at the turbulent water, trying to learn the difference between a harmless standing wave and one that hides a canoe-killing rock. The soothing sound of rushing water also encourages more profound thoughts. I think I'm ready for our impending return to the south. I had intended to examine some personal issues over the summer and bring home specific plans for dealing with them. Nothing has come of this intention. But I've received a greater gift. By temporarily escaping the deep ruts of my well-practiced personal and professional routines, I've been able to glimpse what lies beyond. The view is empowering. I've learned that I'm physically tougher than I had thought and have a higher tolerance for certain pains and irritations. I can act positively in the face of fear and uncertainty, even if I haven't yet learned to embrace them. There's a new sense of confidence. The range of options has expanded, and I'm better equipped to grapple with whatever God puts in front of me upon my return. It's a liberating mental shift, far more valuable than specific answers to specific questions, and I hope it doesn't vanish like this mist, once I'm home again.

Since we're still ahead of schedule, Chris has decreed that we'll sleep late tomorrow and start our paddle at around 10 a.m. We could use the extra rest.

Camp Location: 66° 51.41'N 110° 44.40'W
Distance Today: 23 km. paddle, 2.7 km. portage
Distance to Date: 1183 km. paddle, 46.2 km. portage

Another Hood River rapid.

Emerging from a hole in the Hood River (Chris Morris).

Chapter 21: HELIFISHERS AND HOOD RIVER BAPTISTS

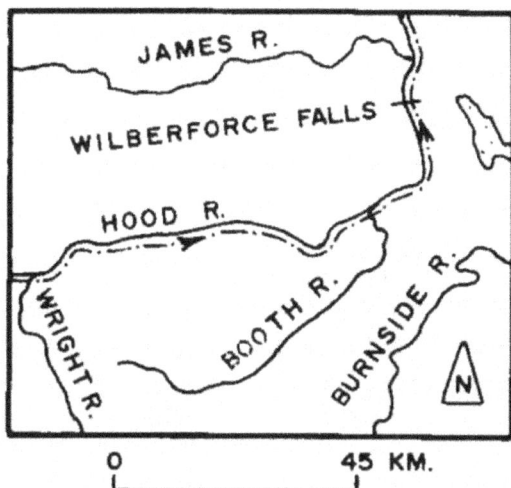

August 16

By rushing water we reclined,
To further sleep committed.
A noisy chopper did arrive,
Two fishermen emitted.
One hour hence, as we contrived
To start our paddling day,
The helicopter reappeared and carried them away.

At 7:50 a.m. on a cool, sunny morning, with mist from the falls wafting peacefully past the tents, our sleep is shattered by a white Bell Long-Ranger helicopter. It thunders over the falls and executes a banking turn above our encampment, the thumping of its blades vibrating the fillings in our teeth. All that's missing is a set of loudspeakers blaring out "The Flight of the Valkyries." This time it's an invasion instead of a reconnaissance. The chopper touches down briefly about 150 yards away, on the opposite side of the river, and two men with rods and tackle boxes leap out like soldiers entering a firefight, completing the conquest of our early morning. The chopper then lifts off with a roar and vanishes above the falls. This must be helifishing, a pricey pastime for the rich and famous. Of course, it could also be a couple of mining company executives or geologists who have decided to play hooky for a while. The sound of the falls and the distance across the river make it easy for fishermen and canoeists to ignore each other, so we do. The helicopter returns within an hour and collects its human cargo. As far as we can tell, they didn't catch anything.

We pull out at 9:45, first paddling across the river to photograph the falls from a different angle. The day becomes sunny and hot, a throwback to the weather we enjoyed earlier in the summer. We run many rapids; I lose count after number five. Most are downstream of the confluence with the Wright River, which enters the Hood from the south. Jill and I decline to run a short, but very rocky Class 2 rapid and make a brief portage, while Chris and Christy, having navigated it successfully, frolic on a sandy beach downstream and take photos of each other.

Most of today's white-water passes without a hitch, but there's anxiety when Chris, after finishing one set of rapids, raises an arm upward, giving Jill and me the signal for "Don't proceed. Pull out and have a look." But we'd already commenced our run. There's much consternation and loud conversation in the boat, but there's no choice but to bull our way through. We skim lightly over a few rocks and power our way through a large standing wave at the bottom with no harm done, except that our disobedience has again aroused the ire of our leader.

While running the last rapid of the day, a large standing wave manages to tilt Jill and me to starboard, almost to the point of no return. We save ourselves only by leaning out and flailing at the water with our paddles. I'm told it's what experienced canoeists call a "brace." To me, it's just an instinctive attempt at self-preservation. As we emerge into calmer water, we see Chris lowering his camera.

Today, we have two separate wolf "encounters of the third kind." The first animal looks at us curiously and then lifts a leg, marking its turf in the traditional way. We don't need the services of Doctor Dolittle to decode this wolfish communiqué: "The mating pair of two-headed, four-armed floaters is advised that this spot is taken. Please go someplace else to lay your eggs, or whatever." Seeking greater acknowledgement and respect, Chris howls at it, but the wolf refuses any further communication, looking at us pointedly for a few more seconds before trotting away. The second meeting is much the same as the first. Unlike the caribou, the wolves up here aren't shy, timid or easily impressed; they seem very self-confident. If we did manage to open a dialogue, I imagine they would ask us, "Who are you and what is your purpose?" Important questions in any context.

We stop at 5:30 p.m., 14 kilometres downstream of the Wright River and 33 kilometres from this morning's camp. I take advantage of the opportunity to wash my hair in an attempt to keep up with the generally high standard of camp cleanliness. It's not a relaxing process. The repeated dousing of my head with ice water causes my scalp to first tingle, then burn and finally, go mercifully numb.

Despite the early hour and the cold water, I'm tired, feeling the effects of post-rapid stress. What affects me most about this river is the casual, indifferent way it tests us each day. There's no malevolence or hostility; there's no recognition or acknowledgement. Sink or swim, do whatever we please, this river doesn't care about us at all. Although we pass its tests repeatedly, there's no exemption from the next round, no time off for good behaviour. The good news is that each rapid lowers our altitude and brings us closer to the sea.

Camp Location: 66° 53.85'N 110° 06.99'N
Distance Today: 33 km. paddle, 0.2 km. portage
Distance to Date: 1216 km. paddle, 46.4 km. portage

August 17

Up at 7 a.m., away at 8 and camped again at 5 p.m., after gaining about 40 kilometres. Once again, we run too many rapids and riffles to keep an accurate count.

In one memorable patch of whitewater, Jill and I finally have our inevitable, involuntary swim. For the record, this occurred at precisely 11 a.m. at 66 ° 55.1 minutes north, 109 ° 43 minutes west. Air temperature as recorded afterward was 62°F. More importantly, the water temperature was 56°F. Here's how it went. After navigating roughly three-quarters of a rocky, Class 2 rapid, we encountered a barrier of rocks too wide to avoid and too cluttered to pass through. Having fallen far behind Chris and Christy and unable to observe their manoeuvres, we were left to work out our own salvation with fear and trembling. We failed. Glancing off the submerged shoulder of a large stone, we were thrown too far over to starboard to recover. We fought the laws of physics for what seemed like a long time using our "brace" technique. Although we lost the battle, we did manage to slow the rate at which we capsized, and the canoe deposited us almost gently into the foaming waters.

It felt peculiar to be evicted from my comfortable seat in the bow of the Wenonah and forced to enter a new, subaquatic environment. I kept my eyes open as we submerged and saw the transition from light of day to murky yellow-green as the canoe became fully inverted. Neither of us got out of the spray skirt until that point, and it took effort to kick and wriggle free. At first, I held on to my paddle, but let it go when I felt I wasn't getting free of the canoe fast enough. When I surfaced, the upended canoe was drifting along beside me, and I wrapped an arm around the bow. Meanwhile, Jill had emerged from the other end with her paddle and clamped herself firmly to the stern. We weren't going to let all that food escape so easily. I saw my paddle floating along in the current a few feet away. Supposing I might need it again, I flailed over, grabbed it and then got back to the canoe. After the initial burst of anxiety caused by the spray skirt, there was no panic. The water didn't even seem that cold. As the boat and its human barnacles were flushed through the remaining turbulence, my primary emotion was a sense of relief: "Now I'm just a piece of driftwood floating down a river. I don't have to pretend to be a canoeist anymore."

Once the boat completed its unconventional run through the rapids, Jill ambitiously got hold of the stern rope and tried to pull our craft to shore, with me still attached to the other end. Meanwhile, Chris and Christy pulled up beside us. After hurried, verbal negotiation, I grabbed the bow of the upended canoe with one hand and the stern of Chris's canoe with the other while Jill held on to Chris's canoe near the bow. The two dry paddlers then worked like dogs to haul the whole aggregation to the north bank, where the wet canoe was righted and the contents removed.

We were in the water for less than 3 minutes. Nonetheless, an anti-hypothermia drill was followed. Dry clothing was assembled and distributed from the still-dry contents of a dry bag. Rich, hot oxtail soup was prepared and administered, along with generous handfuls of chocolate chips, an unexpectedly appetizing combination of fat and sugar. Since Jill and I were as mobile and coherent as usual (maybe even more so, due to our stimulating immersion), the more drastic measure, skin-to-skin contact in a sleeping bag, was unnecessary. The swimmers were warm and dry within 15 minutes, thanks to the combination of bright sunshine, the absence of strong wind, and Chris and Christy's quick work. Apart from Jill's bug shirt, we lost no equipment, and the canoe was undamaged except for a small tear in the spray skirt at the pocket for the spare paddle. We stayed ashore for about one and a half hours all told. During the break, we had a pancake brunch, and most of our wet gear dried out.

The hard part is facing the many remaining rapids to be run this day. We're in whitewater again within three minutes of shoving off. There are no more swims, but some chancy moments. Chris does his best to cheer us up, yelling

"Beans for supper!" as we enter each successive rapid. Beans or no beans, I'll be relieved when, God willing, we've cleared the last rapid on this fast and foamy river. Today's happy news is that there are no portages. Also, there'll be no laundry or bathing this evening, two other cold-water sports I don't enjoy.

At one point later in the day, a figure appears, silhouetted against the sky at the top of the valley wall. It's dressed in black, wearing a large backpack, like a ninja on a road trip. Rather than responding to our friendly waves, it dodges behind some rocks and is hidden from sight. "Do you hear banjo music?" I ask the others, having recently seen the movie "Deliverance." A short time later, the figure re-emerges, this time with two extra legs, curly horns and a shaggy coat. Our "figure" was the hind end of a musk ox, making its way along the valley rim, staring curiously at the two yellow things in the water below.

It may be an optical illusion, but it looks to me as if the very surface of this river has started to slant downhill. Even in the calm sections, the current is fast, which explains the rate at which we're moving downstream. We're now well ahead of schedule, and this may give us the luxury of extra time at Wilberforce Falls, 20 kilometres downstream of tonight's camp.

This evening, so as not to become too engrossed in our own reality, I check my historical notes and find that we're camped at about the same location as Franklin and his party on September 1, 1821. They were working their way upstream, homeward bound from Arctic Sound. Franklin's journal entry, perhaps written on this very spot, contains a bleak summary of their situation:

...on 1st September a fall of snow took place and the canoes became a cause of delay by the difficulty of carrying them in a high wind and they sustained much damage from the falls of those who had charge of them. At the end of 11 miles, we camped and sent for a musk ox and deer which St. Germaine and Augustus had killed. The day was extremely cold...the

thermometer varying between 34 and 36 degrees. In the afternoon, a heavy fall of snow took place. We found no wood at the encampment but made a fire of moss to cook supper and crept under our blankets for warmth.

Once again, I'm reminded that our current trip is just fun and games by comparison.

Camp Location: 66° 54.47'N 109° 08.67'W
Distance Today: 48 km. paddle, 0 km. portage
Distance to Date: 1264 km. paddle, 46.4 km. portage

August 18

We wake to a cold, rainy morning and break camp around 8:45 a.m., stopping a few minutes later to portage a nasty rapid and eat our breakfast. While helping reload the canoe, Jill slides into the river and has to dig out a change of clothing.

Today, it's Chris and Christy's turn to have an intimate encounter with the Hood. A few rapids after breakfast, they strike a rock head-on, puncturing their Wenonah's forward floatation tank and knocking the waterproof case containing our VHF radio into the water, still attached to the canoe by a tether. Chris quickly reels it in, but loses track of his position in the rapid and has to work his way from rock to rock. Welcome to the club! They strike a second rock and overturn, losing the rear part of their spray skirt, a bottle of sunscreen, the camera tripod, and a case containing some of our spare maps. The handle of Christy's paddle is also damaged.

Although we're bounced around and drop over a two-foot ledge, Jill and I manage to stay upright, by the grace of God, and are able to aid in the recovery of Chris, Christy, and their overturned canoe. Ever the leader, Chris issues instructions to Jill and me on how best to accomplish the recovery as he bobs along in the current. A loop in one of the loose ropes is wrapped around his leg, so intermittent silences punctuate his guidance while he ducks below the surface and works to free himself. Christy seems calm as she drifts along beside the inverted bow, damaged paddle still firmly in hand.

Today's weather is not as conducive to swimming as yesterday's; air temperature, measured at the scene, is 52°F while the water is a stimulating 54°F. There's no wind, but it's cloudy. We get the canoe and floating people ashore, and hot soup is again administered, this time by Jill and me to the others, and changes of clothing are again made available. I can't say whether it's more unsettling to be in the water or to watch someone else go over and attempt to assist. Both are stressful, and I hope we're done with these unscheduled, cold-water swimming lessons for the rest of the trip.

Chris assesses the damage to his canoe and decides it's capable of continuing without immediate repair, so onward we go. The day's fun isn't over. No sooner have we returned to the river than we run into the largest standing waves we have yet encountered on this river. Minus the rear half of their spray skirt, Chris and Christy take on a lot of water and have to bail. Jill and I have our bow submerged a few times, and we take on a slug of cold water through the forward cockpit. I'm soaked and must stop for a change of clothes while Jill bails out our boat. So, the river makes good Baptists of us all today. After a short pause, our mad dash down the Hood continues through further rapids. Fortunately, there are no more immersions since we've run out of dry clothing.

Downstream of the confluence with the Booth River, the day's final set of rapids is safely negotiated. A short time later, we pass onto the Arctic Sound 1:250,000 scale map sheet. Here, the gradient of the river decreases, and the stream becomes braided among multiple, gravelly channels. The fast water is confined to shallow riffles, with no large waves and few rocks to avoid. We think briefly about stopping to camp, but the flat, marshy topography isn't very appealing. We've embraced enough water today. No need to sleep with it as well. Continuing downriver, we soon find ourselves at the take-out location for the three-kilometre portage around Wilberforce

Falls and canyon.

As we unload our gear and pitch the tents, we can't fail to notice the five sturdy Royalex canoes already at the landing, along with some piled baggage. Soon, a half-dozen people come marching briskly up the portage trail, members of a 10-day Hood River trip put on by a commercial outfitter from back east. They arrived a few hours ahead of us and have built their camp on a high ridge overlooking the falls and canyon. They're now returning to the upstream end to gather up their remaining equipment, planning to move their canoes tomorrow.

The two tribes mingle cautiously. There's a palpable, awkward dissonance. Most of the others are friendly, but have a hard time believing we've been paddling since July 2nd. They were flown into the Hood about a week ago and are still neat and clean. I wonder how we look to them. I get part of the answer when one woman tells me our canoes look "dangerous." I glance at the careworn boats and then back at her in silence, trying to think of a meaningful reply. My recent, show-stopping rebuttal to Chris would probably not be appropriate here, and anyway, I want to tell the woman my own thoughts on the subject - give her the whole story. I want to explain the pros and cons of the design of our canoes for our purposes. I want to talk about how they carried us so well over such a long distance, and yet sometimes do seem dangerous to me. I want to describe how my boat made me suffer on those early, long portages, yet has become a familiar, daily companion. But I can't refine this disorganized rat's nest of ideas and emotions into the few incisive sentences that the situation warrants. I imagine how my extended response would sound, spilling from the lips of a scruffy, bearded stranger, eyes alight with passion and conviction, a fanatic, a loony. So, I scratch my armpit and say nothing.

After a brief round of superficial conversation, the two groups part company. They attend to their equipment while we continue to spread our wet gear on the shrubs and rocks around camp.

Before departing, the outfitters' guides tell us that they plan to be picked up at the mouth of the Hood on the 23rd. It's now our plan to reach Arctic Sound on the same day. If there's extra room in their aircraft, we can then hitch a ride back to Yellowknife, saving both groups money. Otherwise, we can at least forward a message to Air Tindi's Yellowknife offices, letting them know we'll be available for pickup as of the 24th. This may save us from an extended wait at the Arctic coast. I suspect that when the time comes, we'll be ready to go, unless there's a Club Med up there that we haven't heard about yet.

We cook and eat our meal without much energy or conversation. As a measure of our fatigue, we've not yet taken the time to view the 60-metre-high falls, though the sound of plunging water can be heard just a short distance downstream of camp. May tomorrow be warm and sunny, allowing for lots of good photos and a chance to dry our wet gear. Thanks to God that we're well and whole in this marvellous place.

Camp Location: 67° 05.42'N 108° 47.60'W
Distance Today: 38 km. paddle, 0.5 km.
Distance to Date: 1302 km. paddle, 46.9 km. portage

Chapter 22: The HUMMINGBIRD FROM RESOLUTE

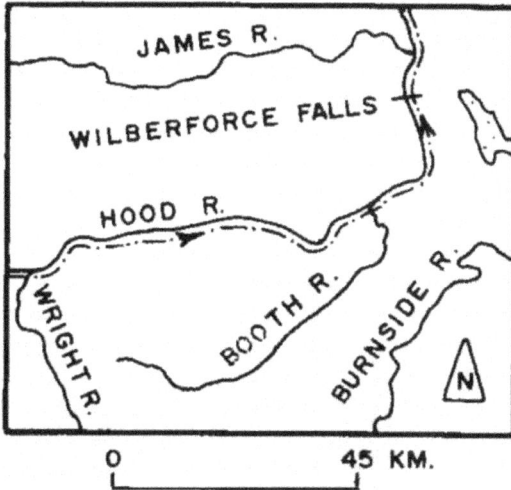

August 19

After a night of intermittent rain, I'm awake at 9 a.m. on a cool, sunny day. As I leave the tent, I hear the magic word, "Snow!" from Jill.

"Where?"

She just points to the hills a few kilometres upstream. Sure enough, their tops and sides are coated in white, glinting in the bright morning sun. Had we been higher up the valley, on time instead of ahead of schedule, we would have had a closer introduction to the end of the short, subarctic summer. Seemingly overnight, the leaves of the tundra's small shrubs and bushes have begun exhibiting their fall colours, predominantly red and mauve, with patches of yellow marking clusters of dwarf birches.

Before Chris and Christy are up, Jill and I take a brief walk along the rim of the canyon and soon reach the falls. These mark the location where the river spills off the eastern edge of the Wilberforce Hills and enters the lowlands at the head of Arctic Sound. Below the falls, the river has worn a slot-like chasm, almost as deep as it is wide. The morning sunshine creates intriguing shadows and colourings within the gorge, and a rainbow glows softly in the spray cast up by the turbulent water.

By 10 a.m., both crews are awake and enjoying a late, communal breakfast of bannock. During the meal, Chris posts the orders for the day: 1) camp will be moved to the downstream end of the canyon; 2) dinner will be served at 7 p.m.; and 3) all gear will be moved to the new camp before dinnertime. It's a more lenient regime than usual, and I have my two loads, including the canoe, over the portage by mid-afternoon. Although the ground is wet in spots, the footing is good, and each three-kilometre passage takes only about 45 minutes. Next, it's time to burn our accumulated garbage. I sit in a sheltered cleft near the rocky margin of this beautiful, remote river, inhaling fumes from burning plastic, trying to make sure that the soggy contents of several large Ziploc bags are fully consumed. Regardless of the setting, I always end up with smoke in my eyes. Once the fire has completed its usual exothermic sterilizing and reducing, I rake the ashes with a stick, collect the non-combustible remnants in a bag and cover the site with deep, wet sand. If I've learned anything at all this summer, it's to never again use the phrase "throw away." There's no such place as "away." No matter where the garbage ends up, someone has to deal with it.

A little later, Jill arrives with the last of her two loads. We converse, and then I crawl into a tent for a nap. I'm disturbed an hour later by Chris' hearty "Hello there!" as he pulls into camp with Christy, their portaging also done. They spent much of the afternoon talking with members of the other group and watching some of them run their empty canoes through the rapids in the canyon below the falls. Chris confesses to having hurled a few M&M chocolate candies down on them from the top of the gorge and complains that they didn't notice. Experts with big egos seldom enjoy watching other experts at work.

I crawl out of the tent in time to see the last group of paddlers working their way methodically through the whitewater, pausing in eddies and picking their way around ledges. I'm struck by the contrast between this display of paddling precision and the bat-out-of-hell style that our own expedition has been using. Part of the difference is explained by equipment. Our fellow travellers, confined to the Hood River, are making use of rugged, highly manoeuvrable Royalex canoes, which can turn on a dime and rub up against rocks without significant consequences. Our long, sleek craft are built for speed, and in speed we must seek our safety. If we snuggle up against a rock, we may crack the thin layer of resin that coats the hulls. We also have a larger turning radius, and attempting to crank our way into an eddy in these tight, boulder-strewn rapids can often cause more trouble than it solves. So, we aim and fire our craft down the rapids, changing direction when we must, and powering through whenever we can. In the future, I'd like to try the paddling style we witnessed today. It seems so calm and controlled. Maybe that woman from yesterday got it right. Maybe our boats do look dangerous by comparison; however, I can say with certainty that our Wenonahs have been just the ticket for covering long distances in comfort and style.

Dinner is held in the cook tent at 7 p.m. as planned. Tonight, it's pasta, cheese and sun-dried tomatoes. It might have been fresh fish, but the latter weren't biting when Chris tried his hand earlier. He did end up catching one small trout. The low temperature, 46°F and dropping, will help ensure that the few fillets are preserved until they're joined by others.

Wilberforce Falls is a popular tourist destination today. Twice, a familiar-looking white helicopter makes low passes along the canyon from north to south, no doubt giving some geologists or well-heeled tourists a bird's-eye view of the spectacle below.

Since we're only about a day's paddle from the mouth of the river, Chris has decreed that we won't paddle tomorrow.

We'll stay at our current camp to make and mend, explore the canyon, or whatever. More clemency! It seems our leader is adopting a more relaxed attitude, now that we're close to our goal. I'm pleased we can afford to spend extra time here. I didn't feel much inclined to explore today after walking nine kilometres on the portage trail.

Camp Location: 67° 06.91'N 108° 49.26'W
Distance Today: 0 km. paddle, 3 km. portage
Distance to Date: 1302 km. paddle, 49.9 km. portage

August 20

Wet snow starts overnight, and we wake up to an accumulation on the crests of the low hills we portaged across yesterday. Winter is literally nipping at our heels. Here in camp, nestled in a protected hollow near the riverbank, the snow is melting on contact with the ground, but as of noon, a slushy mixture of rain and snow continues to fall. The temperature is 42°F, and fog blankets the distant hills. We've had no contact with our more exposed, hill-top neighbours.

For us, the day's main preoccupation is keeping warm and dry. We huddle in the cook tent, sometimes running the Coleman stove to take the edge off the chill. Once again, we thank the anonymous canoeist who left the extra fuel behind at Lupin last year.

After spending the morning in the tepee, I retire to a smaller tent where I can take advantage of my sleeping bag and Therm-a-Rest chair. I'm unwilling to risk getting them wet by dragging them "downtown" to the tepee. I can still hear the murmur of voices there, so I don't feel too isolated, and I've left strict instructions to be notified if food is being served (I'm always hungry these days). It's warmer here in my bag than in the tepee, but if I crave conversation, my priorities will shift again and I'll migrate back to the big tent. It's good to have a choice and great to be under shelter.

There are chores to be done. The handle of Christy's

paddle requires mending, and an inflatable, vinyl bag must be installed in Chris and Christy's canoe, inside their fractured floatation tank. These activities, plus some basic bodily functions, are on hold until the sleet stops. Our schedule will allow us to spend another day here, if necessary, but I'd rather press on and finish the last few rapids and portages. I'm also eager to see the Arctic Ocean; we're so close after having come so far.

Later in the day, a modest cultural event is scheduled. We gather in the cook tent, where Chris reads to us from the Decameron, a 14th-century Italian forerunner of the Canterbury Tales, told to one another by seven women and three men hiding out to escape the ravages of the Black Plague. Most of the tales are irreverent, with much bashing of the established church of the day and jumping in and out of bed with mistresses and friends' spouses. Despite these repetitive themes, the tales are entertaining, and Chris has a fine reading voice. There's nothing as cozy as a good story on a rainy day.

The reading is interrupted by the sound of another helicopter overhead. These days, we seem to attract them like flies to honey. We look at one another silently as the noise swells, fades and then increases again until the ear-popping, thumping roar is directly overhead. Powerless, like the crew of a submarine about to be depth-charged, we wait for the bombs to fall, or the tent to blow away or whatever other scenario our minds can conjure. The noise slips sideways, towards the river. Freed from our paralysis, we poke our heads out of the tent in time to see a large, float-equipped Bell Jet Ranger with the red Canadian Helicopters hummingbird logo on its side, settle on a sandbar a mere 100 metres away. Obviously, but inexplicably, we have visitors from the sky.

As the engine powers down and the rotors slow, we spill out of the tepee and make our way to the water's edge to say hello. We meet Rob, the pilot and his engineer, Scott. They're on their way to Yellowknife from Resolute in the high Arctic, where they've spent the summer recovering empty fuel drums under a contract with the military. The poor weather has forced them to fly at low altitude. Spotting our tents and the adjacent patch of level ground, they chose this location to land and refuel from two small drums in their cargo bay. They jokingly ask if we know the way to Yellowknife and inquire if the McDonald's restaurant at the upstream end of the canyon is still open. We mention that the emblem on their helicopter resembles Canada Post's "winged letter" logo and ask them for our mail. In response, they imply that they have a strip-o-gram to deliver. They're a jovial pair and bring extra life to our camp, which I have begun to think of as Ice Station Zebra and which, as they explain, is now one of the largest settlements between Resolute and Yellowknife.

Rob complains that the weather is rapidly becoming "altogether too crappy for flying." We learn that they've been in the high Arctic since May and are now on their way home, very anxious to make it to Yellowknife via another refuelling stop with our old friends at Lupin Mine. Once the fuel is transferred, they waste no time in powering up and lifting off into the murky sky, taking with them a note Chris has prepared, advising Air Tindi that we'll be available for pickup at the mouth of the Hood River on the 23rd.

A short time later, the big red, white and blue helicopter is back. Apparently, the ceiling is now too low to allow Rob to clear the snow-covered hilltops. Their brief flight was not entirely in vain, because they were able to recover a 200-litre drum of aviation fuel from a cache they spotted north of our camp. This time, when they land, they tie down their aircraft and prepare to wait out the weather.

We offer our guests what hospitality is ours to give. They squeeze into the cook tent along with the rest of us. We serve them coffee, and then cook up a double batch of pan-fried pizza. It's good to be hosts for a change and return some of the hospitality we've received. They seem to appreciate the food, except for the topping of sun-dried tomatoes that Rob unobtrusively picks off and places on his plate. Stomach rumbling, I watch this display of selective appetite with silent amazement. It would be rude to reach over and snatch the discarded toppings from his plate. I'll harvest them later, when I'm washing up.

When Rob learns that Chris has a VHF radio in the tent, he asks to borrow it, explaining that a Twin Otter carrying his client, a military official from Ottawa, is due to pass by on its way back to Yellowknife. He wants to make his client aware of the change in plans so the helicopter isn't reported overdue or missing. When he calculates that the time is right, Rob punches in the general aviation frequency and begins his call. The aircraft is contacted, and we soon hear it pass overhead, a faint drone above the low clouds. After switching over to a company frequency, Rob lets his client know that he and Scott will be delayed. "We're in a tent having pizza," he explains cryptically. The owner of the voice on the other end, probably used to Rob's sense of humour, doesn't pursue this further and instead offers project-related information. As the plane begins to fly out of radio range beyond the hills upstream of camp, there's internal conversation between the pilot of the Twin Otter and the military man. "He's hit the transmit button instead of the intercom," smiles Rob. He keys the radio one last time and gleefully yells, "Wrong button!" There are no further transmissions from above.

After supper, Scott leaves the tent to check something in the helicopter. When he returns, he tries to convince Rob that the weather is clearing. Rob is sceptical, but agrees to fly upriver a short distance to have a look. Chris volunteers to be his passenger, and off they go. They're back 10 minutes later, and Rob declares that conditions are worse, not better. He vows he won't risk death by succumbing to "get-home-itus," an affliction which he claims has killed many pilots in the north. We feel for Scott, who has a wife and two children, he has not seen since the 15th of May. They're waiting for him in Cranbrook, British Columbia. Rob is single with no family concerns. He was born in Burin, Newfoundland, and now lives in Thompson, Manitoba. "A nice town," he says.

We reconvene in the cook tent, where Rob and Scott will spend the night. The ambience is enhanced by Rob's portable CD player and extensive collection of albums, plus a box of chocolates, 4 litres of fruit juice, and a batch of homemade oatmeal cookies freshly baked at the Polar Shelf commissary in Resolute ("Emergency rations," says Rob). Soon, the rain-soaked tepee on the near-frozen shores of the Hood River is rocking to the rhythms of John Prine, Bob Seger and the Waterboys. Talking above the music, Rob and Scott tell us they've spent the past three months flying sling-loads of empty 45-gallon drums from scattered locations in the high Arctic to Resolute, where the barrels were steam-cleaned, crushed and buried. An unofficial secondary task was a quest for narwhal tusks (they didn't find any). They've enjoyed their time in the north, but are also very happy to be heading home. Rob tells us he installed a new patio deck in his backyard last fall and wants to get some use out of it before it gets too cold. Scott is obviously anxious to be reunited with his family.

The conversation in the tepee ranges from technical details of helicopter maintenance to the history of arctic exploration. Later, Rob and Scott go out to their parked helicopter and return with two heavy-duty sleeping bags, extra clothes, and a large shotgun ("Since we're sleeping in the cookhouse," says Rob). They bed down, and the rest of us retire to our own tents.

The wind continues to howl fiercely late into the night, and the rain, snow and sleet continue. The cook tent blows over, damaging the central pole, but our guests manage to re-erect it on their own. Still later, Jill calls to me that our canoes are shifting in the wind and asks for help. Together, we drag them away from the shore and lodge them, overturned, in the shelter of some rocks. I'm of little use since I forget to put on my glasses and am essentially blind.

Camp Location: 67° 06.91'N 108° 49.26'W
Distance Today: 0 km. paddle, 0 km. portage
Distance to Date: 1302 km. paddle, 49.9 km. portage

The Hummingbird from Resolute

August 21

Rain and sleet continue to fall. The river is starting to show the effects of the sustained deluge, rising about one and a half feet overnight. Fortunately, the various tents and vehicles are still high and dry.

There'll be no canoeing today, but there will be flying. Rob decides that he and Scott will take their helicopter southeast to Bathurst Inlet in search of more fuel. They'll then try to work their way to Lupin Mine via the valley of the Burnside River. He thinks that if they can stay low enough, they'll have a good chance of getting to Lupin. From there, Rob sees no difficulty in completing the flight to Yellowknife. We serve our guests breakfast and coffee, and lend them our cook stove to pre-warm their Jet Ranger's gas turbine engine.

While this is taking place, the two guides leading the commercial Hood River trip appear in our camp, looking cold, wet and miserable. We invite them into the tepee, now crammed with eight people. They accept coffee and tell Chris that they wish to use "your helicopter" to get a message to Air Tindi. Due to the adverse weather conditions, they have decided to abandon their plans to reach the mouth of the Hood and now wish to be picked up at the head of the canyon. We give them a pen and paper, and they write their note, entrusting it to Rob. At the same time, Chris retrieves his own note and changes our earliest possible pickup date to August 25. There's no longer a possibility of sharing a charter because the others now need a wheel-equipped aircraft that can use a nearby esker as a runway. We still need a floatplane, because we're determined to end our journey at the ocean as planned. While telling Air Tindi they can come anytime between the 25th and 30th, Chris ends his note with the exhortation, "Come as soon as you can, because it's damn cold!"

We escort Rob and Scott to their machine. A few brief farewells are exchanged as the necessary preparations are made for takeoff. At the last moment, someone remembers to reclaim our stove from the engine compartment of the chopper, saving us from an abrupt change in the quality of our cuisine.

Our other guests witness the departure of the helicopter and then trudge back towards their camp, which they say consists of "a lot of bent tents" due to the weight of wet snow up on the hills. We wonder silently, and not for the first time, why they chose to build their camp so far from water and shelter. Their tasks for the day will include hauling their luggage and canoes back to the upstream end of the canyon and rebuilding their camp. We don't envy them these tasks on a day like this.

Our company taken care of, we cook bannock for breakfast, polish off the last of the air-delivered chocolates and then retire to the tents to do some creative waiting. As of 1 p.m., the wind howls even more authoritatively than before, whipping a cold, biting rain before it. I chew into "The Robber Bride" by Margaret Atwood, but would rather have the Wilbur Smith novel I left back at Vodka Lake. The vicarious, tropical heat of Africa would be a blessing.

Mid-afternoon, the background noise changes. The rain is no longer drumming on the roof above our heads. The gale-force winds and low temperatures continue, but the wind is now an ally, drying out the tents, the packs, and everything else that was soaked by the prolonged downpour.

This evening, Chris reads to us again from the Decameron, another tale of a hoodwinked husband, with lovers sneaking through unlocked garden gates to consummate their affections. It's just like a modern-day soap opera except that the dialogue is much more flowery. At the conclusion of a would-be lover's soliloquy to another man's wife, Chris editorializes, "Puts Hamlet to shame!"

After the reading, a hot topic around the wanigan is the reprimand given us by one of the guides from the other group (we now refer to them as the "hill people"), who accused us of "not shitting at least 200 metres from the river like you're supposed to." Despite all his other pressing concerns — squashed tent, failed trip, double portage — this sharp-eyed weekend warrior spotted a turd and was disquieted enough to tell us about it. He first lectured Christy, and then, in a separate encounter, confronted Chris, never a good strategy. Surprisingly, Chris responded politely until he heard from Christy that she had also been approached. Hearing this, he became less sanguine, vowing to deposit a suitable response on the hill people's equipment. It's hard to account for all the fuss. Many parts of the tundra we crossed this summer hold a greater density of "animal leavings" per square metre than most city parks. I hadn't planned to mention it in my journal, but I've never before seen such an eclectic collection of pellets, patties and logs. To single out a single piece of human excrement, probably deposited by our last night's guests, as worthy of special attention seems shamelessly anthropocentric. We wonder out loud about the origin of the 200-metre rule. Chris suggests that it's the 11th commandment, and we haven't read the Bible with enough diligence.

We plan for an 8 a.m. departure tomorrow, if the wind dies down and the rain and snow don't return. In the meantime, we visit our canoes and do some early preparation. For Jill and me, this includes tying on one side of our spray skirt to save time and bother in the morning.

Camp Location: 67° 06.91'N 108° 49.26'W
Distance Today: 0 km. paddle, 0 km. portage
Distance to Date: 1302 km. paddle, 49.9 km. portage

Wilberforce Canyon.

Greeting the Hummingbird from Resolute.

Chapter 23: A FINAL TILT AT THE HOOD

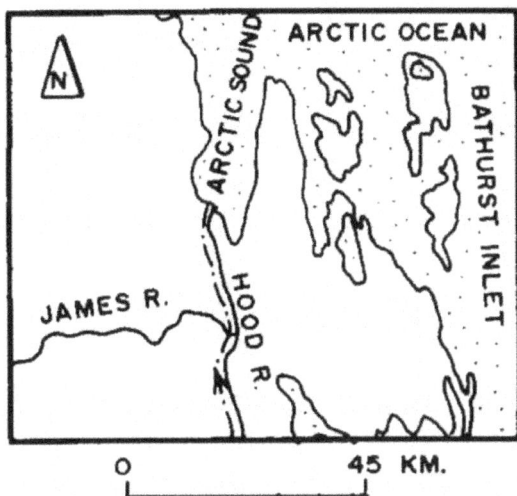

August 22

It's cool and sunny, perfect weather for finishing our journey. We're up at 6:45 a.m., away at 8 and running whitewater by 8:03. We complete three or four rapids all told. In one of them, Jill and I do a repeat performance of an earlier trick: the one where we sideswipe a rock, tilt at a 45-degree angle, flail at the water frantically with our bent blades, and then right ourselves just in time. I vent my usual post-rapid adrenaline in a torrent of words, some of them off-colour. Fortunately, there are no cockpit voice recorders in canoes.

The rapids soon dwindle to a series of intermittent swifts and riffles. Sensing that the end is near, Jill and I forge boldly ahead of the other canoe, scooting through a slippery, boulder-filled spillway with one foot in the boat and one foot out. After we reach deeper water and start to paddle again, we notice a steep drop in the river ahead. Being the lead canoe has its drawbacks. We paddle madly over to the right bank, bruising the Kevlar a bit in the process. Soon we're out of the canoe again, dragging it bodily down another rocky chute. When a small boulder blocks the way, I reach into the cold water, grab the offending lump of minerals with both hands and heave it out of the way. I consider this a small measure of revenge for the grief such misplaced stones have caused us on this river. Chris and Christy follow our example on the opposite bank, minus the boulder heave.

Later, on a calmer part of the stream, we pass through the largest concentration of wolves we've yet seen, five or six on the right bank and two or three more on the left. They're unconcerned, going on casually about their business as we drift by. We howl at them, but apart from looking up briefly, they take no notice.

Further downriver, the water becomes chocolate brown with suspended silt. We also notice a few recent mudslides and submerged vegetation along the riverbanks, evidence of the heavy precipitation of the past few days.

Mid-morning, we arrive at a scenic waterfall, split by a small island in mid-stream. The drop is about 10 feet. We haul our stuff across the island and have breakfast at the bottom end of the portage.

We're making good time, and by about 3 p.m., the last rapid on the river is before us, a wide chute across a bedrock outcrop with a total drop of five feet, followed by a set of standing waves. Chris and Christy line their canoe down the chute and run cleanly through the standing waves. Jill and I decide that we've already given the river ample opportunity to kill us, so we portage the whole damn lot. When it's done, we pause for a snack and hot drinks. I smile broadly and relax, knowing that it's all flat water from here to the ocean.

At 5:45 p.m., as the sun disappears behind a line of grey clouds rolling in from the south, and a cool breeze blows in from Arctic Sound, we reach the ocean with little fuss or fanfare. We ground our canoes on the sandy shoreline below a low bluff on the east side of the river, a few hundred metres from the end of the point that separates the Hood River estuary from Baillie Bay. We've reached the edge of the Polar Sea. Our only remaining task is to hold this position until relieved. Our aerial pickup could come any time from the 25th to the 30th of August. We could be here for as few as two days or as many as eight. But that's okay. We're here. The paddling, portaging, rock hopping, and boulder bashing are done. Regret may come later. For now, lounging in the cook tent after a stomach-expanding, celebratory supper of pasta, salami, dried tomatoes, smoked oysters, chocolate pudding and hot chocolate, I feel only drowsy contentment.

Camp Location: 67° 24.88'N 108° 52.68'W
Distance Today: 39 km. paddle, 0.3 km. portage
Total Distance: 1341 km. paddle, 50.2 km. portage

Jill and I on the Arctic Ocean (Chris Morris).

Cultural relics, otherwise known as garbage.

Ready for take-off: Chris, Christy, the author, Jill.

Trying to hold it in (Christy Simpson).

Chapter 24: DELIVERANCE AND DIMENHYDRINATE

August 23

An overnight rain gives way to light winds from the north, accompanied by low, fast-moving clouds and offshore fog. Despite the return of gloomy weather, we're still in a holiday mood. Wrapped up tightly in my sleeping bag, listening to the sound of the wind blowing in from a strange, new ocean, I stay indoors until mid-morning.

After enjoying a plate of breakfast bannock, I'm off to land's end, spending about two hours exploring the shoreline near the tip of our peninsula. Raised near the seaside in New Brunswick, I haven't visited an ocean coast in a long time. Today, I'm reacquainted with the familiar sound of breaking surf, but the tang of salt air is missing. When I scoop water to my lips, I'm surprised that it tastes fresh. I suppose it's because of the high volume of discharge from the Hood River after the rain and the presence of several offshore sandbars that inhibit the mixing of river and ocean.

The peninsula is a landscape of flat tundra, shallow ponds, frost-patterned ground and string bogs. In the distance, rugged hills bracket the margins of Baillie Bay. Several narrow ravines are carved into the raised bluff on the east side of the peninsula, and communities of small shrubs and bushes have set up shop in these sheltered environments. Seagulls, ducks, ground squirrels, and a few small, sparrow-like songbirds are the visible wildlife. I find the remains of an old camp near the peninsula's tip: two rusty fuel drums, an old boot, two metal cups coated with chipped, white enamel, and a few snowmobile parts. Some would tut-tut about finding this debris in such a remote setting, but I am not at all disconcerted. These relics are a historical record, a story I wish I had the skill to read.

Returning to camp, I'm again confronted by debris, this

time of our own making. I don't need to decipher the tale it tells. I already know all about it. I light the inevitable garbage fire on the sandy beach at the base of the bluff below our encampment, aided by the large quantity of driftwood that has collected here.

Today, each member of our formerly close-knit community is doing their own thing: resting, exploring, or reading in the cook tent. The common purpose that held us together for so long is gone. No sign of rampant boredom or discontent yet; I think it's just that we're each unwinding in our own various ways. I'm sure that Chris, in particular, is happy to be freed from the daily pressures of planning, navigating, patching canoes, and expressing his ego. He's responding by sleeping a lot. As for me, it's back to Maggie Atwood. This diversion will soon be exhausted as I'm already on page 250 of her convoluted tale.

August 24

It's day two of our seaside vacation, and the pleasant, holiday mood persists. We're up at 9:30 a.m. for a scheduled ten o'clock breakfast of bannock, generously marinated in maple syrup. When the bannock runs out, I pop several large chunks of our surplus, naturally-refrigerated butter into my mouth and chew them slowly. The smooth texture and gentle, creamy sweetness make it taste as good as any food I've ever eaten. After that, I head back to the top of the peninsula on a quest for more artifacts. It's great to be able to wander off like this. Later on, we'll have to stay near camp in case our ride to Yellowknife suddenly materializes. That could get tedious.

During today's stroll I find: empty tins of KLIM ("Powdered whole milk"), Old Chum tobacco ("Canada's favourite"), Hutton canned meat, canned butter, outboard motor parts ("Johnson Outboards, Peterborough"), wooden sled runners, a doll's leg, bits of rope and cloth, gloves, various discarded aluminum pots and kettles, the base of a Coleman lantern, and parts of two Coleman stoves ("Do not use ethyl fuel"). It all makes sense. According to the historical notes on my Arctic Sound map sheet, there used to be a trading post about seven kilometres south of here, on the east side of our peninsula. There's also an abundance of caribou bones, so it's no secret what the Inuit were up to at this location: hunting, eating and trading. The variety of the debris suggests that whole families must have lived here on a seasonal basis.

Chris mounts his own solo expedition, deciding to visit the site of the former trading post. When he returns, he reports his discoveries, including rusty bed springs, the remains of a motorboat, and, mysteriously, a single, white, spike-heeled woman's shoe. He claims the latter is evidence that the Transvestite Trapper's Society met at the post on a regular basis. Jill and Christy also take a walk. They don't report their destination or their findings, but later in the day, they retire to the cook tent, talking in low tones and giggling.

Tomorrow is the earliest possible date for our return to Yellowknife. No doubt we'll start hearing aircraft in our minds every other minute. In preparation for our retrieval, we've already packed up the gear that isn't needed on a daily basis and positioned it at the bottom of our bluff. The tents and our personal gear will just have to be collected in a hurry when the time comes. We've set aside a large, empty dry bag, into which we can hurl various unclassified items at the last minute.

I polished off the Margaret Atwood book today. I didn't enjoy it. Maybe it's because I was forced to read and regurgitate so much Canadian literature in high school. Read a novel chosen by someone else and then write an essay about it; I'm glad those days are gone. Chris is devouring the Decameron, but doesn't share any tales with us, promising to read one or two out loud tomorrow. Christy is still chewing through the lengthy biography of Albert Einstein. Jill has started into the Maggie Atwood.

As a small diversion, Chris brings his VHF radio to the supper table and sets it in scanning mode. We soon hear a Canadian Airlines jet 90 miles south of Cambridge Bay, checking in to get a weather report. Chris considers squeezing the transmit button and telling the pilot an off-colour Newfie joke, but refrains. The quality of cultural discourse within our group has fluctuated wildly throughout this magic summer, but I fear that it's now on a sharp, downward spiral. Like pigs in space, even in the stars, we are haunted by the mud.

As another diversion, I build a large blaze of driftwood and incinerate my small, inflatable pillow. Until it sprang an irreparable leak in its fuzzy blue surface, it had been a comfortable nightly companion, but it's of no use to me now. The fierce, reddish-yellow flames yield a tangible satisfaction. It seems my summer of garbage burning has awakened a latent pyromania.

This was another grey day with rain in the morning, which petered out as the day progressed. We had a brief burst of sunshine in the afternoon, but the rain has returned this evening.

August 25

Today, it's bright and sunny, with moderate winds from the south. We meet in the cook tent at 10 a.m. for blueberry bannock and butter. After breakfast, the wind increases, and we dismantle the tent so the crippled central pole doesn't receive any further damage.

Despite the wind, the sun remains bright and the temperature hovers in the mid-60s. Airborne insects are few. We drag out our Therm-a-Rest mattresses and chairs and lounge in the sunshine. Christy and Jill sit together beside the de-masted cook tent. Chris sets up in the shelter of a slight rise near his tent. I lie on the soft, fragrant tundra, a little way off from the others and hope to fall asleep. I've developed a new appreciation for this most basic of recreations.

At 12:30 p.m., there's a distant droning. By the time I'm fully awake, Chris has his telephoto lens extended and is studying the approaching aircraft, a float-equipped single Otter. Still not sure it's ours, Chris decides not to use his radio. He fears that once communication is established, the pilot may decide that he wants to land elsewhere and will tell us that we have to move. According to Chris, if we play dumb, the pilot will be more likely to land at our current location. I'm more concerned that the plane lands at all, but when it begins to circle our camp, we're convinced our expedition is over. Camp is hastily struck. When I next look up, the plane has touched down on the river mouth, taxiing in so close to shore that it disappears from view at the base of the shoreline bluff. Chris hurries to the beach to make contact. He has instilled in us the need for speed, to avoid getting hit with a hefty standby charge by the charter company. Time is money once again, and this air show is costing us several thousand dollars.

Soon, I'm sliding down the sandy bluff with a pack on my back, like a soldier about to be airlifted back to base. Everything is packed and moved to the beach within 15 minutes - very efficient but apparently unnecessary. Our pilot and co-pilot are in no hurry. Collecting us is their only task for the day, and there won't be any standby charge. We unpack the Coleman stove and brew them up some coffee while the plane is loaded in a leisurely manner. We all pitch in to help, trying to lead by example. But the pilots make themselves comfortable on the sandy beach, sip their coffee and question us about our trip, our canoes, and how many fish we caught. So, we squat beside them and counter with questions about their flight, their plane, and our choice of pickup location. They assure us we're in the right place. The water is deep enough and sheltered from waves by the offshore sandbars. Chris asks if they're willing to fly us back along the Hood River, to give us a final aerial view of Wilberforce Falls and the location of Ice Station Zebra. They readily agree. It's our charter, after all.

Our plane is a single Otter, retrofitted with a turbine engine, giving it a sleek, long-nosed look. It's white with red trim and looks very large and businesslike. The pilot has backed it up so that it faces out towards the bay, the rear of the floats resting on the sandy beach. The canoes are lashed to the pontoons, while the rest of the gear is stored inside the cabin, which, as is often the case with aircraft up here, contains a couple of 45-gallon fuel drums and reeks of aviation gas. To smoke in the cabin is to tempt fate.

While I have the chance, I climb back to the top of the bluff for one last look around. With the tents gone, there's no trace of our camp, and I'm hard-pressed to know whether I'm at the correct location.

We climb aboard at 2:15 p.m., after helping the co-pilot push the Otter off the beach. Our Bean boots are all packed away, so we wade out to the pontoons in our bare feet. Engine noise soon makes conversation in the cabin impossible. As we begin to accelerate and bounce across the choppy water, heading southward into the wind, I'm thankful for Christy's thoughtfulness in providing me with her only remaining capsule of Gravol. I'm no stranger to motion sickness and often lose the struggle to avoid the stomach-emptying consequences. Today, the gas fumes will add to the challenge.

We climb and continue south, retracing our route to Wilberforce Falls. As the pilot banks and rolls to please us with the best possible view of the falls and canyon, I snap off a few pictures and then reach for the white bag in the seat pocket in front of me. "Would it help if I tickled you?" Chris yells into my ear from the seat behind. I don't reply, concentrating my mental energies on keeping my bannock where it belongs. I need those calories. I'm comforted by the familiar, dry tingling in my mouth, symptomatic of a strong dose of dimenhydrinate, and soothed by the low temperature of the unheated cabin. The plane levels out, heading southwest, and I fix my eyes on the far horizon, soon recovering enough to snap off a few more pictures. We have a view of Lupin Mine from a distance of about 20 kilometres as we cross Contwoyto Lake. Even from this altitude, the big lake looks choppy. If we were down there today, we'd be bouncing around and getting wet.

We cross the tree line and land briefly at a fishing lodge on Gordon Lake, where the plane is refuelled and the ladies delight in using the bathroom. At 7 p.m., we land on Yellowknife Bay and taxi over to the Air Tindi docks on Latham Island. Our plane docks at the very spot our journey began 55 days ago.

Editor's Note: The narrative ends at this point. Surviving records suggest that among the first tasks performed in town was a pit stop at McDonald's, where large, medicinal helpings of cheeseburgers, fries and Cokes were consumed. This time, nothing was left for the raven.

After Words (2014)

Time has passed, but the reverberations of that subarctic summer continue. Once jolted free of long-established routines and psychological ruts, I wasn't willing to climb back in. I had always known that God would be my rudder, but a rudder is of no use to a ship that stays in port. I'd wasted time, but it wasn't too late. I decided to do some exploring.

Not long after completing the canoe trip, I left my job, a metaphorical life raft to which I had clung tenaciously for too long. I moved to Slovakia looking for work as a freelance English teacher. I had a few adventures and learned a bit of the language. Nerozumiem! Hovoríš anglicky? I also learned hard lessons about the loneliness of a solitary existence in a foreign country. But I didn't find any work. So, I fell down. But I got up again, flying back to Canada after accepting a 2-year contract position with a highway construction project in Atlantic Canada. I swapped my canoe for a kayak and ventured out onto the Atlantic Ocean for the first time. Weekdays, I worked for two different bosses with the same name, but wildly differing expectations of their employees; an adventure of a different sort and more lessons learned. When that ended, I migrated back to southern Ontario and joined the public sector as an environmental planner. I rented part of a house on the edge of Lake Simcoe, allowing for lots of weekend paddling and a couple of more ambitious trips farther north. I even teamed up with Chris for old time's sake, for a helicopter-borne winter camping trip north of Lake Superior. We lived in a tent for a few weeks, skiing, exploring and starting local rumours of a gold strike.

Later, I again felt the call of the east and landed a position with a provincial government on Canada's Atlantic coast. I'm still here. These days, I walk to work along the banks of a river, a longtime dream; no more gut-wrenching commutes on congested freeways. I still take the occasional wander into the wild, including quasi-annual, solo sea kayaking trips along portions of the Labrador coast. But these days, my real adventures are found in human relationships and a part-time ministry with international students, which has led to many new friendships and occasional travel to a distant continent.

I've found my place and purpose. Life or death, I'm equipped for either one. If you don't want this to happen to you, by all means, stay in your comfort zone, avoid risks and dream of retirement.

"And we know that in all things God works for the good of those who love him, who have been called according to his purpose." Romans 8, verse 28.

The author in coastal Labrador, 2013.

References

The quotations and historical context contained in this journal were obtained from the following sources:

Anderson, James. [1855] 1940-1941. "Chief Factor James Anderson's Back River Journal of 1855." Canadian Field-Naturalist. Vol. LIV-LV.

Back, George. [1836] 1970. Narrative of the Arctic Land Expedition to the Mouth of the Great Fish River. Reprint. Hurtig.

Blanchet, Guy. 1964. "Exploring With Sousi and Black Basile." The Beaver, Autumn, 1964.

Christian, Edgar. [1927] 1937. Unflinching - A Diary of Tragic Adventure. John Murray.

Christian, Edgar. [1927] 1980. Death in the Barren Ground: The Diary of Edgar Christian. With an Introduction by George Whalley. Oberon Press.

Franklin, John and Dr. John Richardson. [1824] 1970. Narrative of a Journey to the Shores of the Polar Sea in the Years 1819-1820, 1821, and 1822. Hurtig.

Hanbury, David T. 1904. Sport and Travel in the Northland of Canada. Edward Arnold.

Hearne, Samuel. [1795] 1911. A Journey from Prince of Wales's Fort in Hudson's Bay to the Northern Ocean in the Years 1769, 1770, 1771, and 1772. The Champlain Society.

Hodgson, Maurice. 1967. "The Exploration Journal as Literature." The Beaver, Winter 1967.

Munn, Henry T. 1932. Prairie Trails and Arctic By-Ways. Hurst and Brackett.

Patterson, Raymond M. 1954. The Dangerous River. George Allen & Unwin Ltd.

Pielou, E.C. 1994. A Naturalist's Guide to the Arctic. The University of Chicago Press.

Pike, Warburton. 1892. The Barren Ground of Northern Canada. Macmillan and Company.

Seton, Ernest T. 1911. The Arctic Prairies: a canoe-journey of 2,000 miles in search of the caribou; being the account of a voyage to the region north of Aylmer Lake (1911). W. Briggs.

Waldron, Malcolm. 1931. Snow Man: John Hornby in the Barren Lands. The Riverside Press.

Whalley, George. 1962. The Legend of John Hornby. Macmillan of Canada.

www.ingramcontent.com/pod-product-compliance
Lightning Source LLC
Chambersburg PA
CBHW051824040426

42447CB00006B/365